Spotlight on Communication

Don Robinson and Ray Power

Spotlight on Communication

A skills-based approach

Pitman

PITMAN PUBLISHING
128 Long Acre, London WC2E 9AN

A Division of Longman Group UK Limited

First published in Great Britain 1984
Reprinted 1986, 1989

British Library Cataloguing in Publication Data
Robinson, Don
Spotlight on Communication: a skills-based approach
1. Communication
I. Title II. Power, Ray
001.51 P90

ISBN 0 273 01942 2

Text set in $10\frac{1}{2}$ on $12\frac{1}{2}$ Futura Medium
and 10 on 12 pt Times Roman
Printed and bound in Singapore

Contents

Foreword

From the moment of birth, the process of communication begins and it will continue throughout life as the basis of all human activity.

People communicate in order to impart, convey and exchange ideas, knowledge and information, and do so by speech, writing, pictures, signs and actions. Without communication, society could not exist.

With the rapid advances that are being made in the field of technology and with the expansion and growing influence of the media, people today are being increasingly exposed to new and varied methods and styles of communication. It is therefore of vital importance to acquire the skills needed to cope with a constantly changing environment both at work and in leisure activities.

City and Guilds introduced its scheme in Communication Skills at about the time that the Further Education Curriculum Development Unit was engaged in the development work for 'A Basis for Choice', a framework for pre-vocational courses which includes communication skills as part of the 'core' curriculum. The importance attached to these 'core' communication skills is evident from the fact that they are now being included in the curriculum for most vocational and pre-vocational courses currently being designed for use in schools, in further education and on Youth Training schemes.

One of the main aims of any Communication Skills course is to help the student to develop confidence in his or her own communicative ability. In this book, Don Robinson and Ray Power give students the opportunity of gaining such confidence by imparting information and advice on various aspects of verbal and non-verbal communication. Moreover, they provide practical exercises and tasks which allow students to rehearse the techniques in a range of varied and realistic contexts. The tasks involve the students in a role play and group activities, thus encouraging discussion and the opportunity of learning from each other.

Once students have become confident in the use of these various techniques they should be encouraged to apply them in real-life situations.

Communication skills cannot be practised and mastered in isolation. The material which is presented as a basis for the tasks allows for discussion of such issues as sport, advertising and safety, and should help students to develop an appreciation of how cultural, social and other factors influence communication. It is most likely that many of the topics introduced will be relevant to other elements of the whole course being followed, of which Communication Skills may form only a part.

For many people the teaching of communication skills will be a new venture and it is certain that both experienced teachers and newcomers alike will welcome this book as a tool to help them to devise a more successful course—one in which students will actively participate and one which they should enjoy.

Harry Knutton
Director-General
City and Guilds of London Institute

Preface

This book has been written to meet the needs of young people who have difficulty communicating effectively. It should be helpful to students in their last years at school or for trainees attending sponsored youth training schemes and apprentices on traditional craft courses at college. In particular, the book should prove useful in covering most of the syllabus requirements of the City and Guilds Communication Skills 362 and the communication components of the Certificate of Pre-Vocational Education and Foundation courses. There is also a sufficient range of material to make a reasonable contribution to the needs of first-year technician students and students studying for the BTEC First certificate and for GCSE.

The book is conventional in layout, with each chapter dealing with a recognisable aspect of the subject. Students are invited to attempt fairly straightforward exercises following easy-to-understand explanations and descriptions. Each chapter concludes with some brief practical advice and more substantial tasks aimed at testing, exploring and developing the student's skill in that area. Each task is basically free-standing and there is no intention to present the tasks progressively either in merit or degree of difficulty. Some students might benefit from skipping the text of the chapter and attempting the tasks with only the occasional reference to the text for guidance. We have tried to ensure that most of the exercises and tasks contain sufficient guidance and stimulus to encourage maximum effort.

The book ends with two assignments. These are slightly more difficult to accomplish and they demand a greater degree of group cooperation and decision making.

We would like to thank Elizabeth Shinfield, Rod Pilling, Colin Green, Bob Shepherd, Carole Smith, Mike Amery, Eileen Gibbs, Alex Popowicz and many of our teaching colleagues who have helped with contributions and advice. We are especially grateful to Mike Bickley for his photographs in Chapter 2, and his victims, students of the drama class. Brandon Corns, drama student, drew the cartoons, and the two faces in Chapter 5.

We are grateful to the following for permission to reproduce copyright material:

Bedford Square Press, *Buying a Secondhand Car—Do's and Dont's*
Birmingham Post and Mail Ltd, photographs in Chapter 12
Birmingham Hippodrome
Bournemouth Tourist Centre
GASP
Health Education Council
The Controller of Her Majesty's Stationery Office, *Social Trends* and several leaflets
The Observer
Reader's Digest Association Ltd, tap illustrations and captions from *Repair Manual* in Chapter 12
The RSPCA

1 Why communicate?

Imagine looking into a large room. In the middle of the room, on a plain wooden chair, sits a man reading a book. He looks old, about 60, and one of his shoes has a peeling sole. He appears to be wearing at least two shabby suits, the outer suit bedecked with rows of shiny medals. He is dirty and unshaven.
In the corner of the room, a chained dog is snarling viciously at the man, who continues to read, occasionally lifting his head to smile and to whisper to a blank wall.

If you were asked what this scene communicates to you, what would you say? How would you explain these peculiar circumstances? What is the man doing? Why is the dog snarling? Let us make a list of conclusions we might make:

- The man is poor and destitute because his clothes are shabby.
- He spends a lot of time walking because his shoes are worn.
- It is a long time since he has used soap and water.
- He may be a 'gentleman of the road', or a tramp in plain English.
- He can read and likes reading.
- He seems to be 'off his head' because he enjoys talking to walls.
- The dog regards him as a stranger and a threat.

So far so good. There must be more we can add, but this will be enough for now. The interesting point is that a great deal of communication has taken place yet not a word has been heard or written. We have only looked into a room and heard a dog snarling.

Exercise

What other conclusions can we make?

Using our senses

When we are seeing and hearing we are using our two major senses. The other three, which are less important to humans, are touching, smelling and tasting (some people think ESP—extra sensory perception—is a sixth sense). It is mostly through our eyes and ears, in combination with our ability to speak, that we make contact with each other and learn about the world around us.

This is the amazing thing about all of us. We just cannot stop communicating. We are the victims of our senses. We are automatic communicators. If you find this hard to believe, try *not* communicating with your friends. They will quickly want to know the reason for your silence and what it is they have done wrong. In other words, by refusing to speak or to see your friends you *are* communicating that somehow you disapprove of them.

Defining communication

If we have to define 'communication' we can say that it is the process of transmitting messages between a *sender* and a *receiver*. Unfortunately, this process is not as simple as it seems. Many things can and do go wrong. Often messages are not understood because we fail to speak or to write clearly, or we can't be bothered to read or to listen carefully. If this happens then we get ourselves into all kinds of trouble (like the person who fails to get a job interview because he forgets to sign his name on the letter of application).

It is therefore important for us all to try to improve our communication skills. Above all, we must keep in mind just how easy it is to make mistakes or to misunderstand. We are all intelligent and we should use our intelligence to help us to learn to communicate more effectively.

Getting back to our original story of the tramp in the large room, is it possible that we could all have been tricked? Can we be absolutely certain that he wasn't an actor playing a part and that someone might be observing us?

2 Speaking and listening
Part one

Speaking and listening are *the* most important forms of communication. The human race was speaking and listening long before a single word was written. Writing came on the scene much later.

Speech cannot survive without listeners. Speech, and many sounds that humans make, is meant to be listened to. Of course, we can listen to music or a tap dripping, but we listen most of all to human speech. If we are deprived of this we become deprived ourselves. (Imagine what it would be like if no one talked to you.)

This is an important point to make. Talking is a very *human* activity which binds us together closely. Whatever we pretend to be, we all need human friendship and talking is the chief method we use to get it. This gives speech a considerable power, not only to provide what we need, but a power that can offend and cause distress. However much we want to improve our speaking skills, being aware of other people's feelings is important.

First impressions

It will come as no surprise to learn that speaking is a skill that can be improved. Most of us are conscious of our own worries if we have to speak to an important person or to a future employer at a job interview. Some people are so nervous that they are speech*less*. Others, and there are more than you might think, are so frantic that they can't stop saying silly things they do not mean!

It is important to realise that we make instant judgments about people mainly as a result of what they say to us. It is true that we can dislike someone on sight, but our strong and lasting impressions nearly always come from what people say. Here is a conversation between two car owners:

Driver A: Look, mate, you can't park your car there.

Driver B: Who says I can't?

Driver A: I do. This space is mine. It's outside my house. There's your space over there, outside your house.

Driver B: There's someone else in my space. Anyway, I can park where I like. This is a public road. You've got no parking rights on a public road.

Driver A: Come on, get it moved. If *you* don't move it, I'll move it for you.

Driver B: You touch my car and *you'll* be sorry.
Driver A: And if *you* don't move it quick, you'll be even more sorry.

We will leave this conversation before the sparks begin to fly!

If we think about what has happened here we will realise that two ordinary people have come to the point of a punch-up over a trivial incident within a few seconds. It doesn't matter whether Driver A is in the right or in the wrong. Both car owners have now reached a position where one of them must give way to settle the argument—and perhaps carry a grudge because of it.

Can you see how the car owners got themselves in such a mess? The answer lies in the careless and thoughtless use of speech. If we look closely at what each driver said we might understand how easy it is to get into a sticky situation.

The cause of the argument can be found in the first three lines. Take the first line:

> 'Look, mate, you can't park your car there.'

This isn't the best way to start a conversation. It puts the speaker in a superior position, as though only that person knows where you can or cannot park your car. It may lead the listener to fight back with:

> 'Who says I can't?'

This is a challenge and a threat. The listener refuses to be told what to do and goes on to the attack by challenging the speaker's authority. The first speaker then has the choice either to withdraw his authority or to restate it with:

> 'I do. This space is mine, etc . . .'

The remainder of the conversation gets more and more heated until it becomes white-hot:

> 'And if *you* don't move it quick, you'll be even more sorry.'

The power of speech

This shows how powerful speech can be. It helps us not only to get what we want, but sometimes it gets us into serious trouble. Getting out of trouble, or not getting into it in the first place, requires skill on the part of the speaker. Individuals who have this skill are usually prepared to:

- Let the other person express his or her point of view without interruption
- Make compromises or give way over unimportant matters, and so
- Avoid falling into the trap of being rude or abusive

- Remain reasonably calm, without shouting, swearing or making threatening gestures
- Try to get the other person out of an explosive situation by using *his* ideas as a method of escape. ('I think you might have a good idea there. Why don't we get together and work something out that suits both of us, etc.')

Of course the time will come when your opponent is so stubborn or stupid that you cannot give way any further. Even so, a skilful word-spinner will withdraw before the argument gets out of hand to think over the next move.

Exercise

Go back to the car parking argument and continue the story with Driver B about to speak. You can either write the conversation in your notebook, or act the parts with a friend as Driver A.

Your story will be complete when it has a satisfactory ending, although you must be as realistic as possible.

Thinking

If we want to improve our speaking skills we should try to **think** before we speak. To our close friends we can say almost anything, but to nearly everyone else we should be just a little careful about what we say and especially about the way we say it. Speaking to a police officer, or to an employer at an interview, or to a lawyer, or to someone who is buying from us or selling to us, demands clear thinking *before* we commit ourselves in words.

Exercise

A good friend is to sell his motor bike for £250. What advice would you give him about what he should say or do when the first customer arrives? (Should he be prepared to reduce his price—if so, by how much? Should he point out any technical faults or explain why he is selling? Should he accept a cheque? What else is there to think about?) Jot down your ideas on paper.

Planning

A second useful aid to good speech is a set of **plans**. If you have an important interview or meeting to attend, it is always best if you can prepare some notes about what you are going to say, and if necessary a list of questions you would like to ask. Don't find yourself leaving the meeting realising that you forgot to ask a crucial question!

Exercise

You have recently bought a pair of shoes. After two weeks of wear you notice that the stitching on one shoe is faulty and the sole is about to part from the upper. You decide to go to the Citizens Advice Bureau for advice about what to do about it. Prepare a set of questions to take with you.

Speaking clearly

Once we have decided what we want to say, saying it should be that much easier. Nonetheless, some of us do find it difficult to speak clearly, and so often this is because we lack confidence in ourselves. We also find it hard to accept that we can *improve* our speaking skills. We might believe that we cannot change the way we speak because it is part of our personality. This is *not* the case. We can all improve our **oral skills** if we are prepared to work at it. (Oral = spoken.)

Just as an example, let us take a young woman who is about to answer a difficult question at a job interview. As she begins her answer you notice that:

- She talks so quietly it is sometimes difficult to hear what she is saying
- She has a habit of holding her hand in front of her mouth when she speaks, making it more difficult to hear
- She finds it impossible to look the interviewer in the face and so talks to the table or ceiling
- She tends to apologise for having a point of view and seems unsure of what she is going to say next
- She is unable to complete her answer with ease, taking a nose-dive into a long silence.

Although it is unlikely that any one person would have all these problems even under the pressure of an interview, some of us might admit to at least one of them. If not, we might observe our second candidate. This is a young man attempting to answer the same question. You notice that:

- He speaks so quickly that the words almost bump into one another in a jumble
- Following each gush of words there is a pause for thought, then another gush
- He repeats words and sounds such as: you know what I mean, like; er; um; sort of; and sometimes gives a loud sigh at the end of a sentence as though he is exhausted
- He keeps fidgeting in his chair, poking his finger into his left ear and scratching his nose
- He begins to repeat himself and to answer a question that has not been asked.

Although these young people represent two extremes, they do have one thing in common: they lack confidence in themselves and this is reflected in the way they speak.

There are other kinds of problems. For instance, some people sound boring and lifeless when they talk because they don't change the *stress* on words. If you say 'I feel really hungry' and you emphasise the words 'really hungry' the listener is more likely to believe you.

Many people can talk for far too long and fail to spot those tell-tale signs that show that the listener has had enough (yawning, looking away, tapping fingers). Others find difficulty in starting a conversation because of shyness, or they swear or giggle excessively, or they are misheard because they are not forming their words properly as they speak.

Exercise (using a recorder if possible)

Read aloud this passage. First, try it without emphasis on any particular word, then a second time by stressing certain words to make it sound more convincing:

Don't you talk to me like that. Just who do you think you are. I'm not going to be spoken to like that by anyone, especially you. You mustn't believe everything that people say to you, you know. Why didn't you ask me about it first? We used to be such good friends. Now we seem to be at each other's throats all the time. I wish we could be friends again.

Volume, tone and pace

If you listen carefully to the convincing version of the passage above, you will notice not only the **stress** changing on certain words but also:

- The **volume** of the voice changes, some words are louder or softer than others
- The **tone** of the voice changes, telling us whether the speaker is angry or calm or bored or grovelling, etc
- The **pace** or the speed of speaking alters to give extra meaning to the words

All these qualities (stress, volume, tone, pace) in speech help us to say exactly what we mean.

Helping ourselves

The only satisfactory way to improve our speaking skills is first to identify any problems, and then to practise for ourselves. So if you think you sometimes speak too softly when you feel nervous, get into the habit of raising your voice slightly when you buy something from a shop or when you meet someone for the first time. Begin to look people in the eye when you speak to them, and if you find yourself repeating a boring phrase like 'you know', then stop saying it. Whatever the problem is, you should be able to make some improvements. Above all, try to catch the listener's attention by speaking as clearly and as interestingly as you can.

Exercise

Think hard and critically about the way you speak. Can you identify any problems? If you are working in pairs, can your partner identify any problems for you? How will you try to put them right?

As an experiment, try recording a conversation about what you both did last weekend (keep it respectable) and play it back to yourselves.

8

Tips on speaking and listening

1. **To be polite and sincere when you speak is always more important than the actual words themselves.**
2. **If you suspect that your speaking skills are letting you down it is worth examining them to see where they can be improved. For example, people with a quick temper might decide to walk away or end a conversation quickly before they say something really stupid or unkind.**
3. **It is best to be polite and helpful if you are stopped and questioned by a police officer. Be prepared to answer questions requiring basic information clearly and politely. If you don't want to answer a question or follow an instruction that you think is misleading or harmful you should say 'I don't want to answer that question or follow that instruction before I talk to someone who can advise me'. Don't take on a stubborn silence.**
4. **When it is your turn to listen, give the speaker time to finish without interruption. Ask the speaker to explain anything that is unclear or too complicated.**
5. **If you are at a meeting or in a group discussion, think about what you can contribute when it is your turn to speak. Try to be confident, fairly brief, and clear-spoken. Don't try to hog the limelight.**
6. **Try your best to be a 'good listener'. This is usually someone who wants to listen and seems interested in what is being said.**

The bystander

You are waiting for a bus near a public house at about 11 pm when two men leave the pub and stand next to you in the bus shelter. They seem to be having an argument and are very drunk. The large man is carrying a plastic bag full of potatoes:

Large man:
Now listen, Frank, nobody but nobody is going to owe me money and not pay it back. You owe me 10 quid and I want it back now. Come on, hand it over. Give it to me now. Come on .... Come on ....

Small man:
Lay off will yer. What's up? I gave you the money in the pub. Don't you remember? You've been buying drinks for everybody for the last two hours. Listen George, mate, you've had too much to drink. You've forgotten what's happened. Look at you, look at the state you've got yourself into.

Large man:
(*Sliding down the side of the bus shelter*) I'm tipsy, that's all. I can take my drink. I can take it you know. Right. You've taken my money. Give me back my money. Come on, give it back. (*George slips farther down and is half-lying on the ground*)

Small man:
I'm going home. I'm going to walk back. I'm not getting on the bus with you. You'll get us both locked up.

Frank walks quickly away and crosses the road on a zebra crossing nearby. George picks himself up and grabbing his bag of potatoes staggers after him. Half way across the road George drops his bag and the contents scatter over the road. A passing cyclist travelling from the town centre skids on the potatoes and careers off the road into a nearby portable hot-dog stall, knocking it over and spilling sausages all over the pavement. Meanwhile, Frank returns to his friend.

Frank:
This is ridiculous! George, what exactly are you doing?

George:
Give us a hand, Frank. Help me to pick up these spuds before the law gets here.

Frank:
Don't be stupid man. For God's sake, stop crawling about picking up those things. It's 11 o'clock at night. If yer don't get up now I'm leaving. I'm off. I'll see you.

George:
Come on mate, help us out. I've nearly found them all now.

Meanwhile, a crowd of people have gathered around the hot-dog stall and a pack of stray dogs are eating the sausages and barking at George who is crawling around looking for his potatoes. One dog jumps up at Frank as he helps his friend to get up from the road. The dog bites Frank's hand.

Frank:
Would you believe it! Would you believe it! Now I've been bitten by a stupid dog.

George:
Never mind that. Grab hold of me and let's get lost.

At that moment the police arrive as a result of the general hullabaloo and the traffic hold-up. Both Frank and George are arrested and charged with disturbing the peace. Both plead not guilty and Frank brings a private prosecution against the owner of the dog that bit him.

Rough drawing of the scene

TASK
(statement to be recorded on tape)

As a witness of the events, you are asked to attend the Magistrates' Court to give evidence. There you are asked to explain in your own words what happened. Make a brief and accurate oral statement to the court, without reference to notes, of the sequence of events.

Situations

TASK

10

Everybody gets themselves into a tricky situation sooner or later. Here are some examples taken from everyday life. Working in pairs, select at least three situations from the six examples. First work out who will play which part. The idea is for you to handle a tricky problem without too much fuss, if you can!

1. You are escorting your mother (or father) by train to hospital. She has a bad chest and suffers from asthma. Sitting in a non-smoking carriage you are both joined by a middle-aged man who appears to be the worse for drink. He takes out a large cigar and lights it.

2. Each morning you buy your newspaper from a local newsagent. This morning an elderly woman pushes in front of you in the queue. This is not the first time it has happened to you and you have seen her do it to other customers. You feel that there is a limit to everything.

3. You work for a small company and your supervisor, a Mr Sheasby, appears to criticise your work rather more than he criticises other people's. You have a distinct feeling that he just doesn't like you, although you don't know why. You decide to discuss the matter with him when he is in the process of telling you off for being two minutes late.

4. A very close friend of yours has recently developed an unpleasant smell. You don't know what it is, but you do feel that you ought to say something about it. Your friend has a reputation for unpredictable bouts of anger. Even so, you feel that you are the one person who can handle this delicate problem.

5. You are 16 years old and your parents are complaining about the fact that you have been coming home in the early hours of the morning. Your father in particular thinks that while you are living under his roof he wants you to come home at a respectable time.

6. You share a flat with someone who doesn't do a fair share of the household chores. You have already had a discussion about it, but despite many promises your flatmate has gone back to the old bad ways of leaving all the mess and the washing-up to you. This time you intend to sort it out once and for all.

Skill slot

TASK

The object of this task is to give a short talk and demonstration about any one of the skills listed under the two headings 'Skills in the home' and 'Skills in sport and leisure'. You are expected to explain and demonstrate what is involved in the skill and to encourage your listener(s) to participate.

Your task is completed when your listener has knowledge of the skill involved and can show real improvement in that he or she can actually carry out that skill more effectively than before.

You can choose any one of the following skills or introduce a skill that is not listed, provided it more-or-less involves the same degree of difficulty. It is the speaker's responsibility to organise materials and to get help to make the necessary arrangements.

Remember, having a skill to demonstrate in itself is not enough. You have to think carefully about how you are going to put your skill across to your listener(s). Think first, and then make your plans on paper.

Skills in the home
Mending a bicycle puncture (front wheel)
Wiring a three-pin plug (disconnected from the mains)
Sharpening a wood chisel
Fitting a new tap washer
Washing a baby and changing nappies (using a large doll)
Measuring up for wallpapering
Cleaning and adjusting spark-plugs
Shortening and fitting a bicycle chain
Basic first-aid instruction for home accidents
Darning socks and sewing buttons
Ironing shirts and dresses
Changing a car wheel and tyre knowledge

Skills in sport and leisure
Ball control and distribution in football
Demonstrating a dance routine
Dribbling and shooting in basketball
Simple self-defence tactics for women
Spinning in table tennis
Setting up tackle in coarse fishing
Potting and white ball control in snooker
Serving in tennis
Defensive stroke play in cricket
Putting techniques in golf
Map and compass reading
Explaining the rudiments of chess or similar indoor game

Giving directions

TASK

You invite a friend you met on holiday to your home. You promise to meet her at the main bus or rail station in your town centre and escort her to your home. Unfortunately, because of a sprained ankle, you cannot meet her as arranged, and you phone her to explain how she can make her own way from the town centre to your house.

Record your message on tape. Your friend's name is Caroline.

Café talk

TASK

This is an oral task for a group of four. Each player is first to study the character he or she has decided to play. Think carefully about how you intend to play the part, and about the stress, tone, pace and volume of your voice.

As the script is unfinished, you are expected to continue the discussion in any way you choose.

A conversation between four people: Rod, Joe, Sue and Sid. They are enjoying their lunch in a local café.

Rod:
(*Reading the lunchtime edition of a local paper*) Eh, have a look at this Joe. (*Joe silently reads over Rod's shoulder*)

Rod:
Read it out loud so we can all enjoy it.

Joe:
Well, it's one of the letters: 'Dear Sir, I am so pleased that your paper has taken the lead and exposed this pathetic generation of present-day youth. Many older people, who I like to call the silent majority, would certainly approve of your description of young football fans as 'degenerate'.

'However, I would like to draw your attention to a more serious matter: the total collapse of law and order on the streets of our cities, especially the large number of youngsters who are becoming more and more involved in what is now called 'street crime'. It is virtually impossible for anyone over the age of 30 to walk the streets at night without being 'mugged'. These young hooligans roam the streets like packs of wolves stalking sheep.

'Last week you published an article about the increase in violent crime. It stated that there had been a 90 per cent increase in the prosecution of violent crime in the last 10 years of youngsters between 10 and 18. This proves that young people can no longer be regarded as responsible members of society and only more police and a return to National Service Conscription will stem this growth.

'Right-minded people must stand together.'

(*Pause*) It's a load of rubbish!

Rod:
What d'you mean, a load of rubbish? They wouldn't print it if it was a load of rubbish. They don't print things that aren't true you know. They'd get into trouble.

Sue:
Of course they do. Look at all those stories they print about the Royal Family. According to them they are always having babies when they're not. Most of their stories are exaggerated.

Joe:
But you can't prove that this is true. Where's the proof that young people are responsible for all this? I'm not vicious.

Sid:
Pass the salt.

Rod:
Just look at the facts (*grabbing paper*). A 90 per cent increase in violent crime in only 10 years. That proves it, don't it? You can't have a 90 per cent increase unless people are more violent now than they used to be. That's logic, isn't it. In my day you didn't have youngsters goin' round muggin' the old folks for their pensions, and they didn't have as many free kicks then, neither.

Joe:
Free kicks? What's that?

Rod:
Free kicks. Free kicks, as in football. You thick or somethin'?

Joe:
What has free kicks got to do with anything? We're not talking about football, we're talking about violence. What's free kicks got to do with that?

Sue:
Oh! No! You're not going to talk about football again, are you? I've had enough of football for one day. I've been listening to it all morning.

Rod:
(*Directly to Joe*) It's the same thing, isn't it? Listen, why do they have more free kicks in football, eh? Tell me that. Go on, tell me that. I'll tell you why. It's because the modern footballer plays dirty, that's why. And when he plays dirty, so does the crowd. That's why you have hoodlums on the terraces. They learnt it from the players, and the young players are the dirtiest of all.

Sid:
Have you finished with the sauce? Pass it over. Thanks Jimmy Hill.

Joe:
Look Rod, I don't believe all this stuff about the old days. My old man told me it was the same then as it is now. I mean, we've had two World Wars you know, and what's more violent than that? What's more violent than people shooting one another and dropping bombs on people's heads?

Rod:
That's different, idiot. Your average working man wasn't violent. War's not the same as peacetime. You get told to go and fight. That's different from hittin' an old lady over the head with a bottle. When I was in the army I didn't want to shoot anyone, but I would have done if we were at war.

Joe:
But shooting people is violent.

Rod:
No, not shooting the enemy. Shooting the man who is going to kill you isn't violent, is it? That's self-defence. That's defending your country, too.

Joe:
But what about all those people killed in air raids and in the concentration camps? My Gran was killed in the war when her house was bombed. She wasn't defending anybody.

Rod:
Ah, but that's different. Being killed by bombs isn't the same as being mugged by a hooligan with a knife. He intends to rob and hurt you. Your Gran was just a casualty.

Sue:
But there's more to it than just hurting people. What about all the killing that goes on hunting animals for sport? Killing all those lovely animals. You can't talk about self-defence and defending the country when we let people kill poor animals.

Rod:
But that's different! Killing animals for sport is different. That's not the same as defending yourself against a human who is attacking you.

Sue:
But it's all to do with violence of one kind or another. If you think it's all right for someone to walk about with a gun killing animals, then it makes killing all right, doesn't it?

Joe:
I don't follow.

Sue:
I mean if carrying a gun or doing experiments on animals is OK, then we can't complain if the odd person gets hurt, can we? Having guns makes violence OK, doesn't it?

Sid:
D'you want that cake?

Joe:
Getting back to this letter, what do you think about this idea of conscription? Do you fancy it?

Rod:
Yes. Great. Get the lot of them in the army. That'll sort them out. They wouldn't know what hit 'em. I mean, what's the point of youngsters roamin' about the streets and getting into trouble? Get them into the armed forces and give them a haircut and a good wash. I mean, I saw a bloke the other day with a green stripe on top of his head. His girlfriend had red hair with yellow spots. Together they made a great set of traffic lights. I ask you, what normal people would walk around like that?

Sue:
You are unbelievable! You're just like my parents who think that because we want to do something different from what they did we should be locked up or something.

Joe:
But why shouldn't he have a green stripe if he wants to?

Rod:
Because people with green stripes don't care about what other people think of them. And because they don't care they're not responsible, and because they're not responsible they're going to get into trouble with the law. Is that simple enough for you?

Joe:
Come off it, Rod. You're not saying young people who like to be fashionable are causing the bother are you? I think it's because some of them are out of work and bored. If these kids had something useful to do they wouldn't waste their time causing trouble.

Rod:
Why is it that every time someone gets mugged or their house smashed up by vandals there's always someone else to blame? Why don't you blame the people who did the crime? Look at the 1930s. There were millions of unemployed. There wasn't all this violence then, was there? How do you explain that, eh? Come on, how do you explain that?

Sid:
What's for puddin'?

Rod:
I don't know . . . . Look Joe, I don't take any notice of the papers, you know. They don't influence people as much as you think, and they don't make people believe what they don't want to believe. You're not trying to tell me that what the camera sees isn't true, are you? Did you see the football on TV at the weekend? All those kids running across the pitch and kicking each other's heads in. I mean, I saw it with my own eyes. Thousands of the little sods no more than 12 years old fighting like animals. I'm telling you that it didn't use to be like that, and unless we do something about it we're finished. I agree with that letter. They are all degenerates. We need more discipline.

Joe:
Aren't you exaggerating? There must be reasons why these kids behave like that. I don't behave like that and you don't. It's only a small minority. If they are only 12 then their parents can't be very responsible, can they?

Rod:
There you go again, blaming someone else.

Sue:
He's always blaming someone else.

Joe:
Well, may be we're all to blame. But I don't believe that things are as bad as you think they are. We're as good as you were when your generation was young.

Rod:
Eh! I'm not that old. (*Silence*) Just look at that! (*Pointing to Sid*) He's scoffed all those cakes while we've been talking. Come on Sid, you've been quiet. Why don't you say something?

Continue this conversation.

3 Speaking and listening
Part two

To be a good listener is probably more important than being a good speaker. Speaking in itself is useless unless someone is prepared to listen to us. In fact, all of us with normal hearing have learnt to speak only because as babies we could naturally listen to and copy the human voice.

If listening is so natural, does this mean that we must be equally as good at listening as the next person? Unfortunately, it does not. Some people are good listeners and others bad. Are you, for instance, one of those people who gets into this kind of mix up?

X: Why didn't you turn up last night? I waited an hour for you. What happened? Where were you?

Y: But I did come. It was you who didn't turn up. I waited an hour for you outside the 'Dog and Hounds'.

X: What do you mean, the 'Dog and Hounds'? We didn't arrange to meet there. We arranged to meet on the corner of Deakin Road. We talked about going to the disco there later on. Why did you go there?

Y: Because you said so. I'm sure you said that. We talked about it for ages. Don't you remember?

X: Yes, I remember. But we were going there later on in the evening. I wish you would listen when we make arrangements.

Almost everyone gets into this sort of difficulty at one time or another, and the main cause of the confusion is our unwillingness or our carelessness in listening closely to what is being said.

This is an important feature of listening. Listening is not something that happens to us whether we like it or not. It is an *active* process. We *choose* to listen or not to listen. This explains how we can have a conversation at the same time as the radio is blasting music and the traffic roaring outside. It also explains why some of us are so bad at remembering things like dates, names, place names and travel arrangements. It is mainly because we didn't listen hard enough in the first instance.

Improving listening skills

If it is true that listening is an activity that we control, it follows that we can improve our listening skills by exercising greater control over how we listen. In other words, learning to listen *selectively* might be an advantage to us when it comes to gathering information from a lecture or a talk.

Exercise (to be recorded on tape if possible)

Imagine you are listening to the end of this talk on consumer rights and you want to extract as much valuable information as you can. What are the main points to listen for in this excerpt?

So here we have our friend. Let us call him George. George has a bright idea. He decides to buy himself a shaving brush from a large department store. When he lathers his face the next morning he finds not only soap on his face but most of the bristles from his new brush. Instead of getting a clean shave, our George looks more like a hedgehog. So what should he do about it? The first thing he should do is to stop using the brush and take it back to the shop fairly quickly. If George is a sensible chap he will have kept the receipt and he would take this with him. When he gets to the shop he should ask for the manager and request either another shaving brush or the return of his money. George shouldn't shout or get angry. He should stay calm and quietly insist on his rights. The chances are he will get what he wants. Most shop managers are only too pleased to help customers with a genuine complaint.

Selective listening

If we are thinking seriously about what we are listening to, we should be able to direct our attention on the really important parts and only half-listen to the rest. In this example the key listening points are:

- keep receipts
- stop using the goods if they are faulty
- take back the goods to the shop as soon as possible
- politely insist that the manager replaces the goods or returns your money

If we were taking notes, this is the basic information we might record in our notebooks.

However, most listening and talking occur in face-to-face conversations. This is a conversation between a works manager and a new apprentice:

Manager: How are you finding your new job?
Apprentice: It's all right.
Manager: Are you settling in? I mean, do you get on with the staff here? Are they treating you all right? I take it you've got no serious problems or anything like that?
Apprentice: No.
Manager: What about the work itself? Do you think you will be able to handle the new technology that's coming in? Most of the machines in this workshop have had it. It won't be long before we get the new equipment in. I bet you can't wait to get your hands on it, eh?
Apprentice: Yes.
Manager: You don't sound too keen. These new machines are really fantastic, you know. Once they get going they can really

churn the work out. There could be a big future for you if you are prepared to get involved. Do you *want* to get involved?

Apprentice: (*Shrugging shoulders*) I suppose so.

Manager: Well, it's up to you. I've made enquiries at the technical college about a course for you. There's one running all day Thursday, nine till five, but it does mean an extra evening class as well.

Apprentice: But I go football training on Thursday nights.

Manager: So what?

Apprentice: Well I don't want to miss my training.

Manager: The evening class isn't on a Thursday, it's on a Tuesday.

Apprentice: But you just said it was on a Thursday.

Manager: I said the course was on that day, but not the evening class. Is there something wrong with your ears? Anyway are you willing to attend college?

Apprentice: Yes. Thanks. I'll look forward to that.

Let us take time thinking about this conversation. The mix-up over whether the apprentice was required to attend an evening class on a Tuesday or a Thursday can be seen easily enough. When the manager suggested a Thursday for attending college, the apprentice *assumed* he must also mean Thursday evening. This kind of listening (and speaking) error is quite common. It can and does happen to all of us.

Constructive listening

What should interest us more is the poor quality of the comments made by the young worker to the manager's probing questions. The apprentice doesn't understand how to listen *constructively*. When the manager asks whether he has had any problems settling into the job, the manager clearly wants him to talk about it. This is particularly true when the conversation gets around to the subject of the new machinery. The manager is bursting to have a discussion about it, and he wants to know whether the apprentice is prepared to get involved. The last thing the manager wanted to hear was a feeble 'I suppose so'.

It is easy to accept that the apprentice was unwilling to have a conversation because he was shy or scared that he might say something silly. Unfortunately, keeping your mouth shut at the wrong time or by not constructively joining in a conversation is almost as bad as speaking out of turn!

Knowing what to say and when to say it is more to do with listening than with speaking. You can work out what to say next much better if you listen to and watch the face of the speaker. The speaker will actually guide you into the conversation. If you are prepared to listen and to think carefully about what is being said and the *way* it is being said, when it is your turn to speak you may be surprised how easy it is.

Exercise Working in pairs, re-enact the conversation between the manager and the apprentice. The manager's conversation should more-or-less follow the original wording, but try to experiment by changing the apprentice's conversation in a more interesting direction.

Telephone calls A telephone call enables us to make instant two-way personal contact. Unfortunately, this long-distance method of communicating is so unnatural that many of us feel slightly nervous if we have to ring someone we dont know. Here is an example:

HIGHWAY SPORTS CENTRE

Recreation for all

Interested in sport?
Any sport?
Why not contact the
HIGHWAY SPORTS CENTRE
Instruction available for all sports.
Many teams and leagues already established.
You could join one now!
Get some of your friends and make up your own team!
RING RIGHT AWAY – DON'T DELAY – 457324

Martin saw this advertisement in his local paper. It was just what he wanted. He had been talking to Kenny and some of the other lads about forming a five-a-side football team. He decided to telephone the Highway Sports Centre:

Receptionist: Hello, this is the Highway Sports Centre. Can I help you?
Martin: Yes. Me and some of my mates want to form a five-a-side football team.
Receptionist: Yes, when would you like to book? We've got different leagues on different evenings. Some of the leagues are of a very high standard.
Martin: Well we're not that good. But we're not bad either. Kenny Richards has played for the City reserves.
Receptionist: Yes, I'm sure you're right. But it would be better if you had some idea of the time you wanted to play.
Martin: Well Tuesday would be OK. Hang on a minute, I think Tony goes to the Tech on Tuesdays. He wouldn't be able to come until about half-eight.
Receptionist: I see. Oh! Could you hold the line? I've got another caller.

Two minutes later the pips went. Martin searched in his pockets for another coin. He hadn't got one. He was cut off. Later in the afternoon he met his friend Kenny Richards.

Martin: I rang that Highway Sports Centre. I thought we could get fixed up there for the five-a-side football.
Kenny: What happened? Did you fix it up?
Martin: No, I was cut off. I don't fancy it now. The woman there seemed unhelpful. If they don't want people to use the centre why do they bother advertising?

Exercise

Martin was disappointed. But he could have avoided some of the problems. Write down the errors you think he made.

Planning a telephone call

The first point to remember is that many organisations are often very busy dealing with other callers. This is why it is essential that before you telephone you should know exactly what you want to say. In Martin's case, he had a vague idea that he and his friends wanted to play football, but he hadn't discussed it enough beforehand. He didn't know when the team would be available. He also didn't have enough small change with him—always assume that the call will take longer than you think!

Lack of preparation can cause further problems. This is what happened the day after Martin and his friends decided that they would like to enter the 'Wednesday League'.

Martin: Hello. I phoned the other day about the football.
Receptionist: Yes I think I remember.
Martin: Well we'd like to book a place in the Wednesday League.
Receptionist: Oh! I'm really sorry! The last place has just gone.
Martin: That's great.
Receptionist: The best I can do is to put you onto the waiting list. If there's enough people Mr Jennings said that he'll run another league on that evening. If you want to phone him later in the week maybe he'll be able to help you. Mr Jennings is on a different number. You can get him on 756435. He's the best person to contact. I hope it all works out in the end.
Martin: Yeah. Thanks.

In the evening Martin told his friends what happened:

Kenny: How did you get on?
Martin: I tried to get Wednesday but they were full up. They said we'd have to go on a waiting list. I've got to ring some bloke.
Kenny: Who's that?
Martin: I've forgotten his name. Jenkins or something like that. He runs the football. The woman gave me his phone number, but I've forgotten that too. They must expect you to have a photographic memory.

Exercise

What mistakes did Martin make with his second call?

Well, to begin with he should have been better prepared. He should have had a pen and paper with him to note down important information such as names and telephone numbers. The telephone gives us the chance of fast communication but if we don't prepare properly we waste our time and everybody else's.

What else should Martin have been prepared for?

Rebel Sound
In Concert
Town Hall

Monday 7th October
Wednesday 9th October
Friday 2nd November

Tickets £3 – £2 – £1.50

Box Office open 9 am–5 pm

Phone Box Office 45923
to reserve tickets outside these hours

The recorded message

Karen had been waiting for ages to see *Rebel Sound*. She knew her friend Gillian would like to see them as well. She decided to telephone the Box Office and book tickets.

Box office: This is a recorded message as the Box Office is now closed. Some tickets are still available for the *Rebel Sound* concert. All seats are sold for their performance on Monday 7th October, but tickets at £3, £2 and £1.50 are available for the performance on Wednesday 9th October and tickets at £3 and £2 only for the concert on 2nd November. Please leave your name and address and details of ticket requirements after the tone. Tickets should be collected from the Box Office within 48 hours of this call. Please speak clearly.

Karen: Er. . . Er. . . Oh! I really wanted the tickets for Monday the 7th. That's the day before Gillian's birthday and it would have made a great treat. I don't know what to do . . . I suppose their last concert on the 2nd of November would be really great. They're off to America for their first major tour the following week so they'd want to make it a special night. They'll be in the States for four months. What a pity. The trouble is the tickets are a bit dear. . . I know . . . I'll have two tickets for that concert and my address is 43 Wayside Avenue, Hilton . . . Thanks. . . Thanks . . . Goodbye.

Exercise

Imagine you work at the Town Hall and it is your job to listen to the recorded messages. What problems would Karen's message cause you?

Talking to a recording machine

Many firms and organisations are using recording machines to help those who cannot ring during normal working hours. However, most people feel a little uneasy when they think they are talking to a machine. After all, it is a one-way conversation. The important points to remember are that you have to listen carefully to the message on the machine and to follow the instructions exactly. It's often a good idea to write down in advance your main points so you don't get sidetracked into talking about things that don't really matter.

Tips on using the telephone

1. **If you answer the phone at work give your own name or the name of your company. *Don't* just say 'Hello'.**
2. **If you answer the phone at home just give your home number and wait for the caller to speak.**
3. **Always speak clearly, fairly slowly and politely. If you have a strong regional accent you may have to modify it slightly if you are speaking to someone from another part of the country.**
4. **Try to have a pen and paper handy. Ask the speaker to spell names and addresses if they sound difficult. Write down the details and check for accuracy by reading back aloud. Always repeat telephone numbers.**
5. **Keep reminding the speaker that you are listening carefully by occasionally saying 'Yes' or 'I see' or 'Go on'. Long silences should be avoided.**
6. **If you have to ring someone within a large organisation your call will nearly always be transferred via an internal extension number. Be patient and take a note of the extension number for future use.**
7. **Avoid making morning calls. Ringing in the afternoon is cheaper, and in the evening cheaper still.**
8. **Have a good look at the introductory pages in the telephone directory. They contain a lot of valuable and interesting information.**
9. **The best telephone calls are brief and to the point.**

Small ads

Entire contents of flat for sale. Items include guitar, drum kit, sewing machine, motorcycle kit with helmet, music centre, set of 50 LPs, fridge, cooker, books. Ring 594 0212

TASK

Choose one of the goods advertised for sale and prepare some written questions that will help you to find out as much as you can about the item over the phone.

The telephone bully

Wayne had sent off for three tickets for the *Rebel Sound* concert. In the newspaper advertisement it said that the tickets would be sent within 14 days from the Town Hall box office. After three weeks Wayne began to get worried about the tickets. He decided to telephone the box office:

Wayne:
Hello. Is this the Town Hall box office?

Clerk:
Yes it is.

Wayne:
Well I sent for tickets . . .

Clerk:
Well you should get them within 14 days.

Wayne:
I know that but . . .

Clerk:
If you know that you've no need to worry.

Wayne:
Yes, but . . .

Clerk:
If you have any problems after 14 days please phone again. Thank you. Goodbye.

At this point Wayne heard the telephone go dead.

Wayne realised that some people can be as offhand on the phone as they are face to face. He knew that he had failed to communicate with the booking clerk because he had allowed the clerk to bully him into submission. Wayne accepted that his failure had something to do with his lack of confidence and skill in using the telephone.

TASK

Working in pairs on internal telephones, re-enact the conversation between Wayne and the booking clerk. The purpose of the exercise is for Wayne to find out what happened to the tickets and to get a satisfactory explanation for the delay. Use a tape recorder if telephones are not available.

Personality guessing

TASK

Think of a well-known personality and secretly write the name on a piece of paper. Each person in turn will be asked questions by the rest of the group. Only three answers are permitted: *yes, no* or *don't know*. The point of the exercise is for the group to find the name of the personality with the minimum number of questions.

Think carefully how the questions should be framed.

Shapes

To carry out this task you will need a total of 10 shapes cut from paper or card. These are 2 squares, 2 circles, 2 crosses, 2 triangles and 2 stars each with five points. Each pair should be identical and about 2 inches across.

TASK

Sitting back-to-back with tables in front, one player places 5 shapes in any position on the table in front of him. He then describes their position verbally to the second player who cannot see them. The second player is required to place his identical shapes in the same position on his table according to the instructions from the first player. The two positions should be compared for accuracy after about one minute. You are advised to begin with simple arrangements. The second player should remain silent.

Cars

This is a conversation between two friends, Dave and Phil.

Dave:
Did you go and see that car? What was it like?

Phil:
Fine. I saw it yesterday and I told the dealer I want a couple of days to think it over. He took me for a drive and it felt great, except for a little knocking noise from the engine. He only wants £350 for it. It's a bargain.

Dave:
I don't like the sound of that. Did you ask him what it was?

Phil:
Yes. He said it was a loose bolt or something. He said any mechanic could fix it. Even I could.

Dave:
Did you hear any more funny noises?

Phil:
No, I don't think so. I thought I heard a clonking sound from underneath somewhere, but I'm not sure. Do you know what I mean?

Dave:
No, not really. My dad's got a book from the library on cars. I'll have a look at it before he takes it back. I'll tell you what, I'll meet you tonight outside the park gates. Was there anything else you noticed?

Phil:
Well, I did ask him about the blue steam coming out the pipe at the back, but he told me it wasn't anything to worry about. He said black smoke was the danger.

Dave:
What was the bodywork like?

Phil:
Great! Black and red two-tone. He told me the few small bubbles on the front wing just want rubbing down and respraying. He's going to throw in a tin of paint-spray in the price. He's a great bloke.

Dave:
Look, whatever you do, don't buy it till tomorrow. I'll meet you later on.

TASK

Working in pairs as Dave and Phil.

You are Dave. When you get home you look up the page on car faults in your dad's library book (see below). Read it and work out what might be wrong with the car. When you meet your friend explain from memory what you have discovered and give Phil some tips about other simple checks that can be carried out before purchase. Be prepared to answer any questions Phil might ask.

Check 1 (and perhaps most important) **Rust**. The first thing to look at is bodywork. Gearbox, radiator, suspension, axles and engine can *all* be replaced but once body rot has gone past a certain point most modern cars are good for nothing but the scrapheap. The problem is becoming increasingly acute for two reasons:

- the salt now widely used to clear icy roads speeds up the rate of corrosion
- most modern cars have what is called 'integral' (or 'unitary' or 'monocoque') construction—this means that the body and underframe together provide strength and rigidity (instead of just the frame in a chassis-built car) so that if the body is badly rusted the whole structure is weakened.

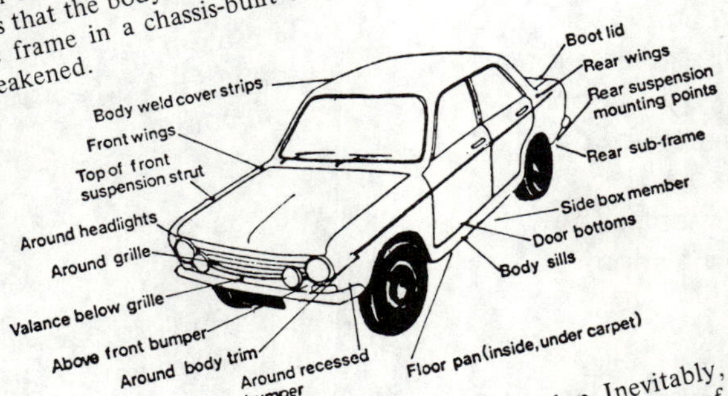

This diagram shows where rust is most likely to develop. Inevitably, you will find a little rust, but be very wary if you find a lot—especially if it's in the form of pimples and blisters.

Even more important than rust which you can see is rust that you can't see, so get the car put onto a lift and look carefully for corrosion at the points where the suspension joins the body and the 'box sections' which run length ways along the sides of most modern cars. If there is extensive body rot at either of these points, *reject the car.*

Check 2 Tyres Check that the depth of tread is *at least* the legal minimum (1 mm), and look for splits on walls (both inner and outer), damage to rims and uneven wear indicating misalignment. Make sure all tyres are the same type (ie all radial or all crossply), and don't forget the spare. Look for plugs in tubeless tyres—they can be dangerous.

Check 3 Wheels After you've looked at the tyres, stoop down at the side of the car facing a front wheel. Grasp it at the top with both hands and shake it to and from you vigorously. A lot of free play or clunking sounds are signs of loose or worn wheel bearings, worn suspension joints or worn steering joints. (This must be done while the wheels are off the ground).

Check 4 Oil and water leaks A few spots of oil under the car aren't sinister, but a lot are. And a leaking radiator usually means a new radiator—not a cheap item. But if the leak is from a perished waterhose, replacement is a simple matter.

Check 5 Suspension Bounce the car at all four corners. When you release it, the car should settle at once at an equilibrium position. If it continues bouncing of its own accord, you can reckon with having to fit new dampers (shock absorbers).

Check 6 Inside the car Check that all the doors open and shut easily and stay open on the hold-open spring, if there is one. Pull back the trim from door edging to see if there has been a respray. Lift up carpets and look for rust. Even a few freckles can mean that water seeps in or soon will. Check for a leaking boot lid—water in the boot can rust through the rear floor. Look at the wear on carpets, seats, upholstery and pedals (the rubbers may have been renewed).

Check 7 Then look at the mileometer reading Does it seem a reasonable one, bearing in mind what you have seen of the inside and underneath? It could have been replaced, tampered with, or turned back to zero, by your dealer or a previous owner or dealer. As a rough guide, 8–10 000 miles per year is the mileage you should expect to find.

Check 8 Lift the bonnet (does it stay up?) Using a cloth, take off the radiator cap gently: If there is an oil slick or rising bubbles, you can expect trouble—at best a blown gasket, at worst a cracked block or cylinder head.

Check 9 Look at the dipstick Don't worry if the oil is dirty, but water drops or greyish foam could indicate a cracked block.

Check 10 Take off the oil filter cap and watch for fuming or smoke. Either could mean extensive wear and might mean a replacement engine.

Check 11 Rev up the engine after it has ticked over for five minutes or so: a worn engine will really belch smoke. Blue smoke is the danger signal for costly repairs, while black smoke may simply be the result of a carburettor fault.

Check 12 Examine the engine compartment for evidence of accident repair, new paint or metal, signs of welding, new suspension, buckling or poor alignment. It should be generally clean under the bonnet, and not too oily.

Check 13 Listen while driving at 40 mph in top gear for a *whine from the final drive* (in the back axle in most cars, in the front where there is front-wheel drive). Now drive at about 30 mph in an intermediate gear to detect another transmission fault—backlash when you sharply depress and release the accelerator several times: *a 'clonk' from the drive axle indicates backlash.*

Check 14 Now test for big end knock. Accelerate up to high revs in any gear, then take your foot off the accelerator without braking or declutching. If there is a dull irregular knocking, the big ends need replacing, which is an expensive repair.

Conflicts!

26

TASK

Here are three outlines of problems taken from real life. Working in pairs and dealing with each problem in turn, choose one of the characters described in the background information. It is entirely a matter for you how to play the part. You are expected to fill in the gaps with your own ideas and words and argue your case as strongly as you wish.

Remember it is a speaking part *and* a listening part you are playing. There are no correct answers, but you must try to reach a conclusion, however unsatisfactory.

You must also decide on your approach to the part. Are you going to be reasonable or unreasonable, aggressive or meek, calm or wild? Are you going to plan in detail or in outline what you are going to say, or are you going to start with only a rough idea and see how it develops? It is your choice.

When the tasks are finished, all the players might like to discuss and explore the reasons why they came to a particular conclusion, and what might have happened if they had approached the problem in a different way.

Trouble at work

A 17 year old apprentice appears to be slipping behind in his studies at the local technical college and making some expensive mistakes in the factory workshop. He is to be interviewed by the foreman.

Background
Apprentice:
Mark Poulson. Mark is having a lot of trouble at home. His parents are going through divorce proceedings and both intend to remarry immediately afterwards. There are arguments about who is going to look after Mark's brother and sister who are still at junior school. Mark has recently been in trouble with the police over minor driving offences and will shortly be appearing in court to face charges.

Foreman:
Mr Beck. Mr. Beck knows nothing about Mark's personal problems. As a busy foreman in a large factory he is very angry about Mark's attitudes towards his work and studies. Although he regards himself as basically a decent person with sympathetic views, he strongly believes that each person should stand on his own two feet and sort out his own problems. Mr Beck himself was an orphan so he knows what he is talking about.

Setting
Foreman's office, 8 am. Mark knocks on the door and enters.

Love story

Eighteen year old Robert Kady is told by one of his friends that Mandy, Robert's girlfriend, has been seen walking through the town centre hand in hand with another young man. Robert decides to speak to her about it.

Background
Robert:
Robert finds it difficult to understand why Mandy is behaving like this. He thought that they had something 'special' going on between them. After all they have been seeing each other regularly for over six months. In fact, he secretly hopes that they might soon get engaged. Robert just wants to know what the hell is going on. There's a limit to what a man is prepared to put up with. Mandy must be told some home truths, but he's anxious not to lose her.

Mandy:
Mandy thinks that being loyal to Robert shouldn't mean being chained to him. She feels that her friendship with him shouldn't stop her from enjoying herself. After all, she is only 17 and you are a long time dead. Just lately she is having doubts about whether to continue their friendship. She likes him very much, but a girl should have enough room to breathe and to have other boyfriends.

Setting
The living room in Mandy's house. Robert and Mandy are sitting alone. Robert speaks first.

Family life

Malcolm Terry has been promoted and his salary almost doubled. He decides to try to convince his wife that this is an ideal time to move house and to live in a better area.

Background
Malcolm:
Malcolm thinks that at last his big break has come. Out of the blue he has been promoted from the factory floor into management. He feels that their little terraced house, which they share with one child and a dog, is no longer the sort of house a works manager should live in, especially now another baby is on the way. He knows that his wife is going to oppose him.

Diane:
Malcolm's wife, Diane, knows what he is up to. She has heard it all before. Why should they move? Why don't they spend the extra money building an extension? This house is so convenient for shops and schools and buses. Last time they discussed moving house she threw a cup and saucer at him. Diane feels nice and comfortable in their little house. Her mother lives in the next road and they have good neighbours and friends in the locality. She is going to take a lot of persuading!

Setting
Malcolm presents his wife with a small but expensive gift to mark the occasion of his promotion. This would be a convenient time to bring up the subject of moving house.

The brush-off

Sandra was feeling anxious. She was expecting her old boyfriend to phone. The last time they had met she told him clearly that she didn't want to see him again. But he wouldn't take no for an answer. He had phoned twice while she had been out and he had written a couple of letters. In the last one he said that he would phone on Friday evening at eight o'clock. Sandra didn't want to be rude or unkind but she did want to make sure that Tony didn't call her again. When the phone rang she picked up the receiver nervously. She tried to compose herself for the ordeal.

Sandra:
Kingsly 7659.

Tony:
Hello Sandra, Tony here. I wonder if you fancy going out tonight?

Sandra:
No I can't this evening Tony. There's a film on Channel Four I want to watch.

Tony:
I just thought we could pop out for a quick drink or something.

Sandra:
No, I'm sorry. I've got some work I've got to do for college.

Tony:
I thought you said you were going to watch a film?

Sandra:
I'll do the homework before the film starts.

Tony:
Come on Sandra. Just a quick drink for old time's sake.

Sandra:
I'm sorry Tony but . . .

Tony:
I've just had the photos back. D'you remember the photos at Pat's party? I thought you might like to see them.

Sandra:
I would but . . .

Tony:
Well I'll come round then.

Sandra:
But Tony there's no point . . .

Tony:
You want to see the photos, don't you? You've just said you did.

Sandra:
I know but . . .

Tony:
I'll be round your place in half an hour. I won't stay long. Promise. Bye.

The phone went dead. Sandra felt depressed. She didn't want to be rude to Tony but she wished she had got the message across to him more effectively.

The problem with the way Sandra handled the conversation was that she had failed to exert control. She had allowed herself to be drawn into a conversation about the photographs taken at Pat's party. Tony, who was far more skilful in getting his way, took control of the conversation to his advantage.

When we answer the telephone we have to be prepared to think quickly and intelligently, and to avoid the temptation to say things (or not to say things) we might later regret.

TASK

Consider the situation Sandra is in. Where do you think she went wrong? Working in pairs on internal telephones, re-enact the conversation between Tony and Sandra. Tony is determined to see Sandra again and Sandra is equally determined not to see him. Do not feel restricted by the original conversation. You may allow the conversation to develop in any way you wish. Use a tape recorder if telephones are not available.

Finding out information

TASK

With the help of a telephone directory or the Yellow Pages find out the names, addresses and telephone numbers of the following places which are reasonably near to where you live:

- A garage equipped to conduct MOT tests on cars
- The local Police Station
- A driving school
- A hospital
- A TV repair shop or TV service engineer
- A travel agent
- A technical college

4 Speaking and listening
Part three

30 The job interview

There can't be many people who enjoy being interviewed for a job. Sitting in that room waiting to be called into the manager's office is enough to set the strongest heart pounding. For a minority, actually having to come face to face with the interviewers is enough to stop the heart completely!

Yet this is the moment when final decisions are made. You have filled your job application form accurately or your personal letter of application has been well received. You have now reached the last hurdle. Whether or not you get the job will depend on the impression you are about to give your questioners. Let us listen in on part of an interview:

Manager: We have dealt with most of the straightforward questions. Now I would like to ask you about yourself. I notice that you have written on your form under hobbies that you go fishing. That's a pretty unusual hobby for a girl, isn't it? Tell me more about this.

Applicant: Yes, I'm keen on fishing. Sometimes I go fishing twice a week.

Manager: Tell me more about it.

Applicant: Well, I go with the club. It's organised proper like.

Manager: Go on, tell me what happens. Give me some details.

Applicant: Well, we leave about six in the morning, get to where we're going, get out the equipment, and fish. That's all.

Manager: I see (*pause*). Can you explain to me why you applied for this job?

Applicant: I saw it in the paper.

Manager: Yes, but there were several jobs advertised. Why did you apply for this one?

Applicant: Because I'm out of work, and my friend told me this is a good place to work.

Manager: Can you think of any other reasons?

Applicant: Well, the money looks all right. I thought the wages looked reasonable, so I applied for the job.

Manager: So you didn't apply because you thought working here might be interesting?

Applicant: Oh! I see what you mean! Yes, I suppose so. Yes, I would be interested in working here. The job seems to be quite interesting and I think I might enjoy doing it, although I would like to know more about it.

Manager: Well, fire away.

Applicant: What do you mean?

Manager: Perhaps you would like to ask me a specific question about the job?

Applicant: Well (*pause*). I just can't think of a question for the moment (*pause*). Could I ask one a bit later on?

Manager: Can't you think of just one question you would like to ask me now? Ask me the first question that comes into your mind.

Applicant: Yes. What are the chances of doing any overtime? Do you get paid extra for working over hours?

Manager: I don't know the answer to that. We will have to see whether you are suitable for the job before we talk about overtime.

As you can see, this particular applicant has made some fairly basic errors. To begin with she has failed to understand that an interview is a two-way process. She is as much entitled to interview the manager as the manager is entitled to interview her.

The manager also expects her to be more responsive to his questioning. When he asked for details about her hobby he was eager to get a constructive answer. He is probably not in the least interested in fishing, but he is interested in whether the applicant can talk intelligently and fluently. Some employers believe that participating in a sport helps to build character and gives the person an idea of what it is like to work in a team. This is important when you consider that most jobs involve working with other people.

The most crushing question the manager asked was 'Can you explain to me why you applied for this job?' This is called an open-ended question because there can be more than one answer—in fact, there are dozens of possible answers. The manager is not necessarily looking for the perfect answer (no one knows the perfect answer) but he is interested in the way she handles a difficult question. The reply 'I saw it in the paper' or 'Well, the money looks all right . . .' might be honest answers but they are not good answers because they make the job sound like any other job the applicant might have applied for. The manager wants to hear that she particularly wants *this* job because it is special to her.

Perhaps her worst mistake was her unwillingness to ask a question for herself. Not asking suggests a couldn't-care-less attitude, a lack of initiative. The manager was forced to press for a question, and he got for his trouble 'What are the chances of doing any overtime?' If our friend was ever in the running for the job, this was the moment she lost it.

Exercise Working in pairs, re-enact the interview. Convince the manager that you are the best person for the job. You will need to improve your interviewing technique.

Preparing for the interview

You can help to improve your chances of success by taking a few simple precautions before the interview. Here is a checklist:

1. **Find out as much as you can about the employer's business. What does the company make or sell? Do you know any employees who could provide you with any inside information? Go to your careers officer or teacher for advice. Ask around generally.**

2. **If you have been told where the interview is to take place, try and visit the premises beforehand if it is not too far. Note how long it takes to get there. Iron out any snags in the travelling arrangements.**

3. **Think about how you are going to present yourself. Neat business-like clothes are best—but don't overdo it by trying too hard to make yourself look older or more sophisticated than you are.**

4. **Think about how you are going to deal with those tricky open-ended questions. For example:**
   - **Why do you think I should offer you this job? (A very common question)**
   - **What are your weak points? (This is a nasty one)**
   - **Tell me something interesting about yourself.**

5. **Prepare some questions that *you* can ask so you are not caught off guard. Suitable questions might include:**
   - **What kind of training will I be given?**
   - **What hours will I be expected to work?**
   - **When would you expect me to start work?**

6. **If you are invited on a pre-interview tour of the premises, take an active interest in what you see. During the interview you might like to ask a question about it:**
   - **I noticed a new machine being installed on the first floor and I wondered what it was.**

The interview

To be late for a job interview is a mistake. Arriving on time, sitting quietly in the waiting room, not smoking or chewing, and knocking on the door of the interviewing room before you enter, are the least you can do to help yourself. Once you are in, you are on your own.

Although there are lots of theories about how you should conduct yourself during an interview, the following advice should be helpful:

1. **Be yourself. Don't put on a false front by playing hard-to-get or by being too smart. On the other hand, being withdrawn and shy can suggest a lack of confidence and initiative. Try to strike a balance by being quietly confident and friendly.**

2. **When you enter the room, close the door quietly and wait until you are offered a chair. Take a sitting position that suggests you are interested in the proceedings. Don't flop into the chair like an old sack or sit bolt upright with your arms folded and legs crossed.**

3 **Look at the interviewing panel as naturally as you can. Always look at the person who is speaking to you. Staring out of the window or looking at your shoes gives a bad impression.**

4 **When it is your turn to speak, look directly at the person who asked the question. Try to talk to him or her as naturally as you would talk to anyone else.**

5 **Answer questions as honestly as you can. Don't show off by exaggerating your abilities because experienced interviewers can see through this.**

6 **Unless it is required, avoid Yes and No answers. Answer questions as fully and as interestingly as you can—but know when to stop.**

7 **If you are asked a really difficult question, give yourself time to think about the answer. Don't be panicked into saying something you don't want to. Don't lose your dignity or your temper.**

8 **Keep in the front of your mind the idea that the employer is looking for someone who is prepared to put a lot into the job—interest, enthusiasm, hard work and ability.**

9 **Be prepared to ask questions yourself. Questions about wages and holidays and time-off should not be the first questions to ask. If you haven't been told the basic details, ask 'Can you give me details about wages and hours?' Don't ask 'How much are you going to pay me for what?'**

10 **When the interview is finished, it might be in your interest to say something like 'Thank you for your time and trouble'. Leave the room without fuss (don't leave anything behind like documents or umbrellas) and close the door quietly behind you.**

There are usually two methods of being told whether or not you have got the job: by letter or by being called back into the interviewing room to hear the good news.

Further interviews

Being interviewed for a job is not the only kind of interview you are likely to be involved in. If you work for a large company you may well be asked to attend what are called **appraisal interviews**. These are designed to find out, mainly through a friendly talk, how well or badly you are progressing in your job. If you continue to do well you may eventually get promoted.

Other kinds of perhaps less attractive interviews include disciplinary interviews at work, interviews with police officers, solicitors, Town Hall and Job Centre officials and Social Services staff.

Whatever form the interview takes, we should always try to prepare ourselves for the ordeal as best we can.

Tips on interviews

1. If you can afford it, get together an appropriate set of clothes for your first interview. Keep these clothes for interviews and special occasions only.
2. Before you leave home for the interview check that you have got all the documents you need, and a pen.
3. If you do suffer from nerves, it is best to jot down on paper any questions you would like to ask and take these with you. Sometimes during an interview the mind can go completely blank!
4. Don't be surprised or worried if you are asked to complete pre-interview tests for aptitude and intelligence. Employers do not necessarily select candidates with the highest score.
5. During the interview, be prepared occasionally to address people by name. Some people are pleased if you can remember their names.
6. Don't be too disappointed if you fail to get the job—it may have nothing to do with your performance at the interview.
7. Try to learn from failure. If you have made mistakes, try to put them right next time round.
8. Be ready to ask for travelling expenses, especially if you haven't been successful.
9. Some interviews for jobs can be very informal. You may be interviewed in a noisy workshop or over a car bonnet or inside a busy shop. Don't lose sight of the fact that you are still being interviewed by being too casual with your answers to questions.

Wanted

WANTED

We are an expanding company who are looking for an intelligent and hard-working young person to work in the garage office and forecourt.

Realistic wages paid. Losses deducted from wages by arrangement.

Ring for an appointment:
Sanshope Garage 581 6633

TASK

A close friend of yours has been invited for an interview at the garage.

Make a list of at least six crucial questions your friend should ask at the interview.

Dispute!

The problem

Barry Jones, an 18 year old apprentice, throws a paper cup of tea at a vending machine which appears to be faulty. The machine has not been working properly lately and many employees have been losing their money or getting drinks they did not want.

The foreman, Ron Crump, sympathises with Barry and asks him if he would mind cleaning up the mess he has caused. Barry refuses to do this and tells the foreman 'to get lost'. The foreman repeats his request and reminds Barry that he will be forced to take serious action if he refuses a second time. Barry tells the foreman to 'stick the machine where he wouldn't show his mum'.

The foreman sends Barry home for the rest of the working day with instructions to report to the manager's office at 8 am prompt the next day. Barry puts on his coat and leaves the factory with the words 'and I shall have something to report too'. Ron Crump reports the incident to the works manager.

TASK
(for 3 people)

You are Mrs Margaret Henderson, the works manager. Barry Jones is sitting outside your office waiting to be called in. You have jotted down four points that seem to be important:

- How shall I deal with Barry Jones?
- Shall I pay him wages for the time lost?
- What shall I say to the foreman?
- What else is there to do?

When you have thought through how you intend to handle the problem, you are ready to ask Mr Barry Jones to step into your office. Mr Crump is also available for interview. The responsibility is on your shoulders.

Preparing answers

TASK

Write out in outline suitable replies for any three of the following questions:

1. Why should I select you for the job in preference to the other applicants?
2. What do you think are the most important qualities an employee should have?
3. Why do you want to work here?
4. If you do get this job, how will you go about making it a success?
5. What is the most interesting thing you have ever done in your life?
6. What kind of books or newspapers or TV programmes do you like best?
7. What do you think management is for?
8. Supposing your parents left this area to live abroad and you wanted to carry on working here, how would you go about reorganising your life?

The job interview!

TASK

36

For this task you have the choice to be either an interviewer or an interviewee. When you have made the choice, read the instructions below.

Instructions for the interviewing panel (3 members or more)

As a member of the management team in a large supermarket store you are to select the best person for a job in junior management. You have also arranged for the advertisement opposite to appear in the local newspaper.

Preparing for the interview
Before the interviews begin the panel must discuss the details of the job. What exactly is the job? What kind of person do we want? What training will be given? What are the wages, conditions and prospects? You must put yourself in a position where you will be able to answer the candidate's questions. It is best to elect a panel leader to take overall control.

The next job is to read through the application details for the six candidates and plan your questions. It is most important to make your list of questions before the interviews begin. When devising questions, don't ask rude or pointless questions such as: 'Have you ever been divorced?' or 'How old are you?' (you should know) or 'Will you work hard if you get this job?' (can you imagine anyone saying No!). But *do* ask difficult questions such as: You don't like your present job, so why should you like this one?

The interview
It is best to conduct each interview in a quiet and friendly manner and never to bully or harass the candidate. It is your job to find out whether the candidate is suitable for the job. When you ask questions, give the candidate time to answer and don't be satisfied with trivial or evasive answers. If you aren't satisfied with an answer, keep pressing. Give the candidate an opportunity to do plenty of talking.

After the interview
After each interview you should discuss the merits of each candidate and complete *one* column on the interview checklist (see page 37). When all the interviews are finished you are ready to make a decision. If you want to recall any candidate to answer further questions you may do so. All candidates should be informed of your decision. (Think about how you are going to do this.)

A traineeship in retail management

An established and successful chain store is looking for a young person to train in retail management.

The person will be between 16 and 19 years of age, well presented, and eager to learn about the retail business. The work will involve duties as sales assistant in the first instance.

Good training will be given and attendance at college is required.

Ring 356 2241 for particulars. Ask for Mr Jameson, Personnel Manager.

Interview checklist

How do you rate the applicant in the following:

Enter scores in the columns as 1 = poor, 2 = average, 3 = good

		Sonia Jackson	Steven Ray	Surjit Kaur	Gary Stevens	Darren Lewis	Roberta Jinks
1	General appearance						
2	General attitude						
3	Overall impression of the candidate						
4	Quality of answers given						
5	Quality of candidate's questions						
6	Suitability of qualifications						
7	Past work experience						
8	Personality						
9	Ability to work with other people						
10	Keen to do a good job						
	Totals						

Name of candidate with highest score:

Instructions for the interviewee

You are to be one of the following six candidates on pages 38–43 and you are eager to get the job. Read through your application form and familiarise yourself with the details. It may be necessary for you to invent further details to sound convincing. You must put yourself in a position where you will be able to convince the interviewing panel that you are the best person for the job.

Be prepared to think about the kind of questions you might be asked and the way you intend to answer them. Also think about and produce a set of questions you intend to ask them. Are the questions intelligent? Are they appropriate? Good Luck!

Instructions for interviewing panel

When you have completed each interview, discuss the 10 qualities above and record your scores under each candidate's name.

When the checklist is completed you will have an idea of the best candidate. You may or you may not regard this person as your final choice.

Application details for Sonia Jackson

Age	16 years 5 months
Status	Single
Present occupation	Unemployed
Previous experience	Part-time paper girl for 18 months at school
Education	Randall Hall Comprehensive. O-levels in English, French, History. CSEs in Home Economics, Geography, Maths and Science
Interests/hobbies	Dancing, singer in Reggae band, music and cooking
Personal details	Partial blindness in left eye because of childhood accident

Reasons for application
I have always wanted to work in a shop since I was small. I have tried to find work in this area but I have been unsuccessful because there are no jobs anywhere. I have worked on a paper round for my local newsagent and he let me serve in the shop on Saturday mornings. I hope you will give me an opportunity to show you how well I can work and I will be glad to attend college for further training.

Reference for Sonia Jackson
As head teacher I was responsible for supervising Sonia's studies during her last two years at school. Sonia was a quiet girl who spent a great deal of her time alone, although she was very loyal to her few close friends. She was an average pupil who succeeded in gaining some useful qualifications because she was prepared to work very hard. I felt that there were times when she was unwilling to join in group activities such as sport and school outings, although it is possible that shyness and not pure awkwardness was the cause.

Marjorie Trainer
Headteacher

Application details for Steven Ray

Age	17 years 6 months
Status	Single
Present occupation	Storeman in large supermarket
Previous experience	Worked part-time in uncle's second-hand shop when younger
Education	Myston High School. O-level in Maths. CSEs in Art, English, Science and Religious Knowledge At present attending college for typing and technical drawing
Interests/hobbies	Writing short stories, swimming and ice-skating
Personal details	Convicted of entering a warehouse and stealing a pen when 13 years of age

Reasons for application

I was very happy working in my uncle's second-hand furniture business and I was sorry when he had to close. I feel I am in a rut in my present job and see no hope of getting to a higher position for many years. I am very interested in the retail trade. I like working with the public I like the challenge of buying and selling. My ambition is to become a retail manager in a large successful chain store such as yours.

Reference for Steven Ray

As Steven's last form teacher I found him a pleasant person. He was very conscientious and had a good record of attendance and punctuality. Unfortunately, he once associated with a gang of boys who led him into crime, but he has now recovered and is working hard to overcome this blight on his record. I feel given the opportunity, Steven will go far in the retail trade. He has a knack of getting on with everybody and was very popular at school.

Dave Thomas
Form teacher

Application details for Surjit Kaur

Age	17 years 7 months
Status	Married
Present occupation	Working as a shop assistant in parents' grocery shop
Previous experience	Part-time working in parents' shop
Education	Randall Hall Comprehensive. O-levels in English and History. CSEs in Geography, French, Science and Maths.
Interests/hobbies	Dressmaking and cooking
Personal details	At present lives above her parents' shop with her husband and baby

Reasons for application

Although I am working in a successful family business I feel that I am not using my full potential and I feel stifled. I know that given the right opportunity and position I could be an asset to such a company as yours. I enjoy meeting people and I am used to working hard. I am also an honest person and used to handling money in my parents' shop.

Reference for Surjit Kaur

I have known Surjit and her family for many years. They are a law-abiding and hard-working family. She is a bright and confident girl and she wants to further her education. I feel in a situation such as you are offering she will be able to succeed. You will not be disappointed if you employ this girl.

Dr Gurmit Singh

Application details for Gary Stevens

Age	16 years 10 months
Status	Single
Present occupation	Unemployed
Previous experience	Six months working in Hant Colliery as a miner. Made redundant.
Education	CSEs in Maths, English and Science
Interests/hobbies	Computers and fishing (coarse)
Personal details	Usual childhood illnesses. Broken left arm in sling

Reasons for application

I know now since leaving the pit that it wasn't the life for me. I am ready to face a new career in a different type of employment. I like working with people and I think I can organise well. I became interested in the management side of the pit while I was there but I could see no opportunity for advancement for many years. I feel your situation could offer me that opportunity. I could be of great value to your company if you give me a chance.

Reference for Gary Stevens

Gary is a very ambitious young man. I could see the potential in him. He would have been ready to step into my shoes when I retire in a few years' time. He was a great loss to the pit and it was a pity redundancy came along and claimed him first. He will go far if given the right opportunity.

Graham Hunt
Manager

Application details for Darren Lewis

Age	19 years
Status	Married with one child
Present occupation	Sales assistant in gents outfitter
Previous experience	Labourer on construction site (5 months), British Army (6 months), Pipe-fitter (8 months)
Education	Fairfield County School. Parkson Technical College (1 year course). O-levels in History, Maths, English, Economics and Geography.
Interests/hobbies	Reading, politics and snooker
Personal details	The candidate said he preferred not to complete this section.

Reasons for application

I would be very pleased if you would give me an opportunity in management. I have had several jobs working with my hands as a craftsman and I feel the time has come for me to use my intelligence in a more demanding occupation. I think that handling people is the most important part of management and I think that I could do well in this area. If you are willing to take a chance on me I will be prepared to work for only half pay until you are satisfied that you have made the best choice.

Reference for Darren Lewis

Darren worked here for about 7 months as a pipe-fitter trainee. He was a good worker with a friendly attitude towards his workmates. When he was given a job to do he was the kind of person who would get down to it and would not be satisfied until he had done a good job. He sets himself very high standards of craftsmanship and finds it difficult to produce second best. Because of the urgent nature of our business we both agreed that it was advisable for him to find a job of a more demanding nature.

James Updike
Foreman

Application details for Roberta Jinks

Age	17 years 1 month
Status	Single, but shortly to marry
Present occupation	Unemployed
Previous experience	Hairdresser 1 year
Education	Hargrave Comprehensive. CSEs in English, Art, History, Geography and Home Economics
Interests/hobbies	Listening to music, jogging and TV
Personal details	Skin allergy and slight asthma

Reasons for application

Although I haven't got a job at the moment, I am very keen to work in a shop again. I liked working with the public and I got on fairly well with the customers I used to serve in my previous shop. If you will give me a chance I will be willing to work hard and learn all I can about the retail trade. I also look forward to going to technical college for training and I promise to work hard at my studies. If you contact a Mrs Warrilow at my previous job she will vouch for me as a good worker.

Reference for Roberta Jinks

I was Roberta's supervisor at the 'Scissors and Curls' Hairdressing Salon in the High Street where she worked as a trainee hairstylist for one year. She was forced to leave when she developed a skin complaint because of all the chemicals we use in the job. She also had a bad cough which was made worse with cutting hair. She was a good girl, very punctual and hard-working, with a lovely friendly manner. I was so sorry when she had to leave. If you can find a way to take this young lady on in your store you won't be sorry. She is a good little worker.

Mrs Warrilow
Supervisor

5 Speaking without words

Writing and speaking involve arranging words in a meaningful way to enable us to pass on information to each other. But we are often involved in communicating without using words. If you were to ask someone to describe you from the expression on your face as you read this book they would no doubt say that you were 'concentrating'. (We hope that you are not looking bored!) Similarly, if you walked into a room and saw someone seated like the person in the following photograph, you might think that he too was concentrating. No words need be spoken. You don't have to write or to listen to anybody. You *know* just by looking at him.

Imagine you are walking down a street and you see a friend coming towards you. As your friend approaches you see that she is upset. When she comes nearer, you know from the expression on her face how you will greet her. You would no doubt ask her whether or not she was all right. Not only do people's facial expressions tell us how they are feeling or the mood they are in, but they also give us clues about how we should talk and deal with them. If you saw that your friend was upset it is highly unlikely that you would tell her more bad news.

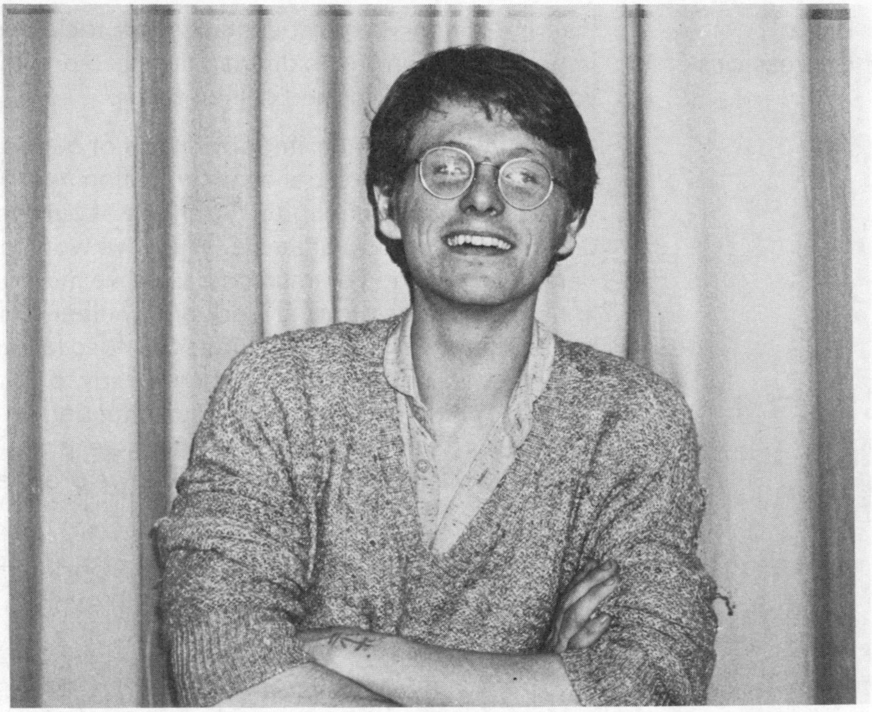

From this photograph you can tell that the person is happy, that he is approachable, and any conversation with him is likely to start off in a friendly and good-humoured manner. The happy mood is passed on to us through *non-verbal communication*.

Exercise

Look at the following photographs. Briefly describe what 'message' you think is being communicated. Compare what you have written with a friend's description and see where you agree and disagree. Note down what led you to make your judgment.

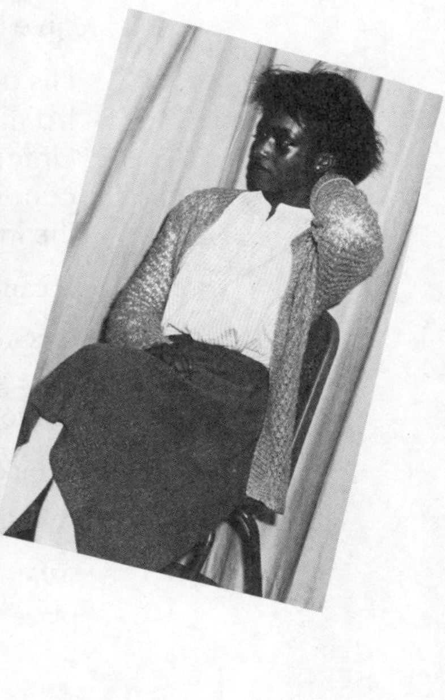

Facial expressions

In terms of non-verbal communication, facial expressions are very important. When you examined the three previous photographs you no doubt first looked at their faces.

Our faces are the most important part of our bodies when it comes to expressing non-verbal communication. Almost without thinking we are constantly changing the shape of our faces to reflect our different moods and attitudes. When we want to know what a person is trying to communicate to us we must always try to look at their facial expressions to work out whether their words ring true. Sometimes we have to see a person's face to know that they mean what they say! For example, when we say to someone 'Have you any idea what I really think of you?' that person can only know what this means by the way we say it and the expression on our face. Our face will tell the listener whether we are friendly or hostile.

Exercise

Using what you consider to be the appropriate facial expressions indicate the following moods. Test your expressions by asking a friend to identify them:

- puzzlement
- happiness
- worry
- surprise
- anger
- disgust
- indifference
- confidence

Non-verbal signals

If it is true that we can know about people by watching them closely, it must also be true that other people know a lot about us. The way others see us will be determined by the non-verbal signals we communicate as well as the verbal signals. Here is an example:

John took a lot of time and trouble with his job application form for Hadley Electronics. He made sure he answered each question and gave plenty of reasons why he wanted the job, including a list of hobbies and interests. He hoped that his application form would give his prospective employer a good impression of him.

His application form did indeed make a good impression with the training officer. John was sent a letter inviting him for an interview. Unfortunately, he didn't get the job. On paper he seemed an ideal candidate, but his behaviour at the interview let him down. After the interview he told his sister what had happened.

'I can't understand it. I felt sure I was the right bloke for the job.'

'Oh well,' Ann said, trying to cheer him up, 'I suppose something must have gone wrong at the interview—or maybe they thought the job wasn't for you. Have you thought of that?'

'You could be right, but I suppose I got off to a bad start.'

'What do you mean?' Ann asked wanting to hear more.

'Well I was 20 minutes late. But Hadley Electronics is a really difficult place to find. It's right at the far end of the trading estate.'

Ann didn't say the obvious. She remembered the letter John had received from Hadley. It had stressed that plenty of time should be allowed as the Hadley building could prove difficult to find.

'What sort of questions did they ask you?' Ann asked.

'Questions? If that's what you call them. The training officer asked me if I was tired. I mean what sort of question is that to ask anyone?'

'Well, there must have been a reason.'

'I suppose I yawned a couple of times when he was telling me about the history of the company. I was up late the night before listening to the new *Rebel Sound* album at Dave's. I didn't get home till about two.'

'I'm not surprised he asked you if you were tired then.'

'Whose side are you on anyway?' protested John.

'I'm on your side of course. But you were supposed to make a good impression. That's what interviews are supposed to be about. At least we put your suit into the cleaners in plenty of time, so you should have looked smart at least.'

John blushed. Ann looked at him. He was wearing his scruffy old jeans and battered trainers.

'You did get your suit out of the cleaners?'

'Well,' John's face was very red now, 'I meant to get it out but I went into *Rockin' Records* to see if they'd got the new *Hunches* single and then I met . . . .'

Ann cut him off before he went any further.

'You mean you turned up like that? In those jeans and trainers?'

'Yes. But what's wrong with the way I'm dressed? Nobody cares that much about dress these days.

'There's nothing wrong with your clothes if you're just loafing about. But come off it John, not at an interview.'

'It's stupid,' John protested, sounding as if he knew he had a weak case.

'But you know as well as I do that you make an effort to smarten yourself up when you go out somewhere special. I mean when you went to Rick's wedding you spent hours getting ready.'

John didn't say any more. He didn't need to. His face said it all. He knew that although he may well have been the best candidate for the job on paper he had talked himself out of the job without having said a word.

Exercise

1 List the mistakes John made in his approach to the interview.
2 Supposing you were the training officer at Hadley, what impressions would you have formed about John on the basis of his behaviour?

Gestures

We often make gestures with our hands and arms to communicate with each other in the normal course of living. Waving goodbye to a departing friend or holding out the arm to shake hands are obvious examples. Use of the hands and arms in a more controlled way is also an effective way of giving instructions. We are all familiar with the police officer at the traffic lights directing traffic when the lights have failed. While this might look fairly easy, the officer has to make each gesture clear and precise so that all the road users understand the signals. We sometimes use gestures to communicate with each other in situations where we cannot be heard properly such as in a noisy workshop or when our listener is a long way off. Deaf people have mastered the art to a high degree with their sign language. Frustrated motorists, too, have their own unique way of communicating silent abuse!

Look at the following photograph and work out what the person is doing:

When we use gestures to communicate we have to make sure that the people we are communicating with understand what we are doing.

Exercise Using gestures show how you would communicate the following:

- You want someone to keep quiet
- You want someone to hurry up
- You are helping a friend to back his car into a garage
- You want someone to speak louder because of the noise
- He's crazy
- Get away from here
- Shut the door quietly and come over here and sit by me
- You're late

Posture Here is an extract from a report on a football match between Fenton Rovers and Boulton Harriers:

> If the first half was quiet the second half exploded as soon as the Rovers' striker kicked off. White, weaving through the Harriers' defence, was brought down. The resulting free kick was well saved by Lyle. Then came the breakthrough. Henderson broke through on the wing and centred a low ball to Newton, and he hit the ball first time. It had hit the back of the net before the Rovers' keeper saw it coming.
>
> You couldn't help feeling sorry for the goalkeeper. He has played in three semi-finals before, and as his team-mates prepared to kick off there was something about the way he stood on the edge of his area, head down and frowning, hands on hips. He seemed to sense another defeat. He said more in that moment than he would have done in a thousand press interviews.

The reporter at the semi-final between Rovers and Harriers was commenting on the posture of the goalkeeper. He was indicating the mood of the keeper from the way he was standing. In the same way, we might be able to guess from a person's posture if he is dejected, bored or happy. In the following photograph you can see that the person is frightened:

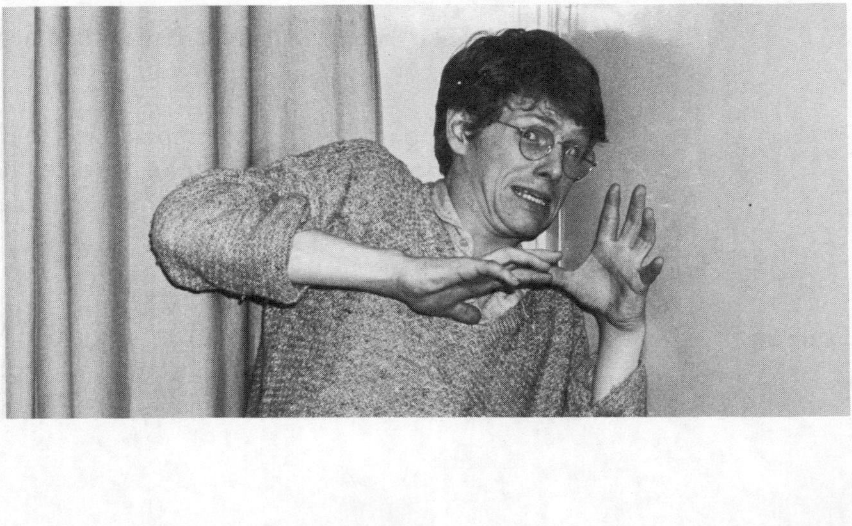

In the same way we are aware of our own posture when we hold ourselves erect when paying attention. We wouldn't sit slumped in a chair or sit nervously on the very edge of the chair with our arms folded at an interview. We want to look as interested as possible and the way we allow our bodies to communicate information is often as important as what we say.

Exercise

Using posture or body language show how you would communicate the following:

Standing

- I am extremely sad
- I am very angry
- I am casually waiting for someone

Sitting

- I am really interested
- I am bored
- I am very nervous

Proximity

Gesture, facial expression and posture are all part of non-verbal communication. There is one other aspect we need to consider. Read the following passage and you will get some idea of what this is:

> Mike was sitting upstairs on the bus. He had the upper deck all to himself. He took his newspaper from his pocket and started to read the sports pages. After a few minutes, the bus pulled up at a stop and through the window Mike noticed his mate Alan getting on. He knocked on the window to attract his attention. Mike was looking forward to having a chat. Alan usually had lots to say for himself.
>
> When Alan came upstairs Mike was surprised. His friend sat at the opposite end of the bus. 'Hey Alan, what's the matter with you? Have I got the plague or something?'
>
> 'Oh it's you,' Alan replied, pretending not to have noticed his friend.
>
> Mike saw Alan turn round in his seat and face the other way. He was obviously upset about something. He wanted to keep his distance in more ways than one.
>
> Oh well, Mike thought to himself, if that's how he feels I'll go back to my paper.

Alan was using non-verbal communication to point out to Mike that something was wrong. His tone of voice, the way he looked at Mike, and the position he took up when sitting on the bus all added up to a powerful message.

Exercise

Look carefully at the photograph on page 51. What is taking place? Do you think these people know each other? Explain the reasons for your answers.

We know from our own experience that in the company of strangers we normally try to maintain a certain distance between them and us. Just how near or how far we like to be is what is meant by proximity. With friends we tend to stand closer to them. We feel confident and safe because they do not pose a threat or offer a risk of any surprises.

Remember when you were last in a crowded lift? People often feel uncomfortable in such situations. This is because they are huddled together with strangers. This is why you see individuals averting their eyes from the person next to them to stare at the ceiling. They use their eyes to indicate that they don't like to be in such close proximity with strangers.

Tips on non-verbal communication

1. **Always remember that we often tell people something about ourselves through gestures and facial expressions without realising it.**

2. **You may have unconscious non-verbal habits which annoy people, such as failing to look at people when they are talking. Sometimes we might look bored when we don't mean to, and this can lead to problems. Think of how you present yourself to others and ask: 'Is this the image I want people to have of me?'**

3. **Gestures can take the place of oral and written communication and can at times accompany these more usual forms of communication. Make sure that when you are using gestures they are clear and that you are getting the right message across.**

4. **Always take into account that non-verbal language is sometimes difficult to interpret accurately. For example, a contorted face may be communicating grief and mental distress or it might be a sign of stomach ache. We need to make use of our other communication skills before we say something silly or unkind.**

First impressions

Donna and Phil were talking about the first time they met. It was at a twenty-first birthday party of a mutual friend.

'I remember seeing you in the corner. I think you were with Tommy and I thought you were a real poser,' Donna said laughing.

'What do you mean?' Phil asked, wondering how she had seen him like that.

'Well you were holding that glass of wine we were all given when we first got there and you were trying to look really cool and casual.'

'I can't remember that at all. How do you mean I was trying to look cool and casual? It amazes me you could tell all this and we hadn't even said a word.'

'It's hard to explain,' Donna said, 'but you can tell . . . .'

TASK

Describe the gestures and posture you think Donna would have noticed about Phil at the party. What other 'images' do people try to give through non-verbal communication?

Conveying feelings

TASK

Write down some situations from everyday life where a person might feel threatened by the presence of strangers.

TASK

Speak aloud one of the following statements. Then by changing your facial expressions, gestures and tone of voice repeat the statement to give it a different meaning:

- Have you got any idea of what I really think of you?
- I want my money back
- Put it over there
- Come here
- What are you looking at?
- I don't want to see you again

TASK

Convey one of these statements effectively without using words:

1. I'm hungry and I want you to give me something to eat and drink.
2. I'm tired and I'm going upstairs to bed.
3. I want to go swimming. Do you want to come with me?
4. You can't come in here—go away or you will be in trouble.

Now write down a similar statement of your own and continue with the task.

TASK
(with video and playback if available)

By changing and moving your posture show that you can become:

1. A very old and feeble person entering a room.
2. Utterly depressed and shattered by some bad news.
3. Confident and commanding in the presence of inferiors.
4. Excited and nervous about a forthcoming event.
5. Physically threatening towards an opponent.
6. Meek and frightened in the presence of physical danger.
7. Friendly and welcoming to a newcomer.
8. An interviewee entering a room, walking to a chair and sitting down in preparation for a job interview.

Interpreting gestures

TASK

Think of an occupation and write it on a piece of paper. Using non-verbal methods of communication try to communicate the occupation to your friends.

TASK

Look carefully at these photographs. Write down in your notebook a brief description based on your interpretation of what is happening. Also write a short thought 'bubble' for each individual in the photographs.

TASK

When we look at someone, we often find it difficult to actually tell from their expression or posture what they are thinking or what mood they are in. This of course doesn't stop us guessing. Often we have to make assumptions if we are to know how to approach the person.

Look carefully at the following photographs and write down two brief interpretations of what each person might be thinking and feeling and what action is taking place:

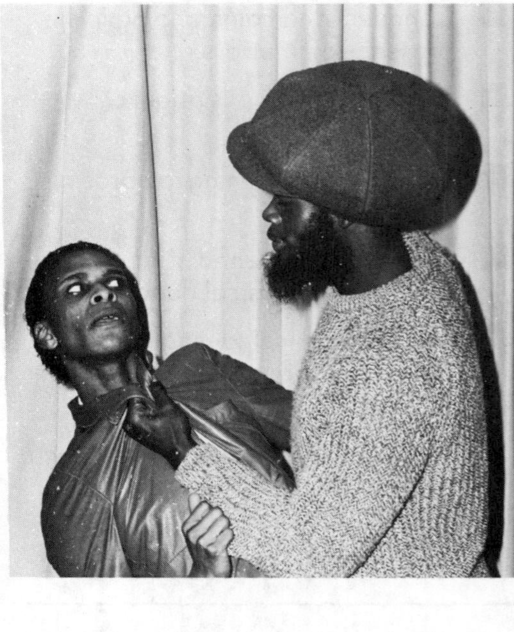

Reading expressions

TASK

In your notebook write down what you think these two men might be thinking.

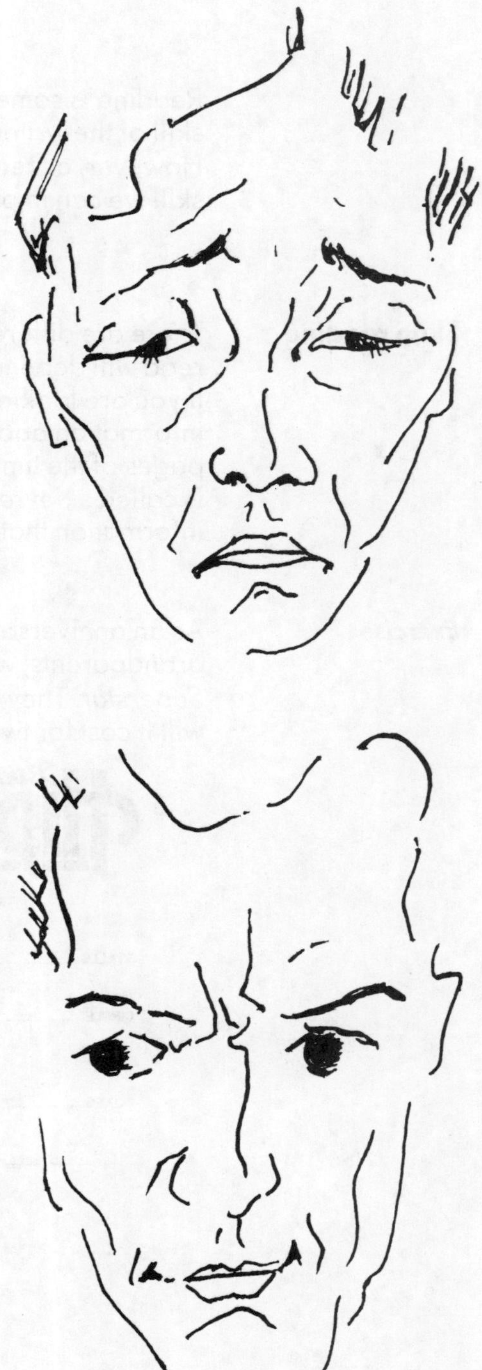

6 Reading and understanding

56 Reading is something we do alone and usually we can rely on the skill of the writer to communicate his thoughts clearly to us. However, as readers we also have to use our skills. Reading is a skill we can improve only with practice.

Skim reading

There are different ways of reading, and the way we choose to read will depend on what we are reading and why we are reading. If you are looking at a bus time-table you will only want to read information about the bus you want to catch. You will skip through pages of the time-table until you come to the service you want. This is called *skim reading*. With skim reading the reader will want information that is going to be of use to him.

Exercise

As an anniversary treat you want to buy two tickets for your grandparents, who are both pensioners, for the show *Jesus Christ Superstar*. They want to go on a Wednesday afternoon. How much will it cost for two tickets?

Birmingham
HIPPODROME

Theatre Director:
RICHARD JOHNSTON
Theatre Manager & Licencee:
BARRY HOPSON
Box Office:
021-622 7486 (4 lines)
Party Booking Line:
021-622 6043

TICKET PRICES

	Adults	Children
STALLS	£8.00	£6.00
	£7.00	£5.00
	£5.50	£4.50
CIRCLE	£8.00	£6.00
	£7.00	£5.00
	£5.50	£4.50
	£4.50	£3.50
	£3.00	£2.50
BOXES	£36.00 (for 4 persons)	
	£32.00 (for 4 persons)	
	£24.00 (for 3 persons)	
	£21.00 (for 3 persons)	

CONCESSIONS

PARTY PRICES (20 or more)
Available for all Performances except Saturday evenings

		17–26 Aug		28 Aug – 11 Sept	
	Normal Price	Special Adult Party Price	Special Children's Party Price	Adult Party Price	Children's Party Price
STALLS	£8.00	£6.00	£5.00	£6.50	£5.50
	£7.00	£5.00	£4.00	£5.50	£4.50
	£5.50	£4.50	£3.50	£4.50	£3.50
CIRCLE	£8.00	£6.00	£5.00	£6.50	£5.50
	£7.00	£5.00	£4.00	£5.50	£4.50
	£5.50	£4.50	£3.50	£4.50	£3.50
	£4.50	£3.50	£2.50	£3.50	£2.50

SENIOR CITIZENS
(except Friday and Saturday evenings)
Monday to Thursday £4.00
Matinees £3.50

STUDENTS
(except Friday & Saturday evenings)
All seats £3.00
ALL CONCESSIONS SUBJECT TO AVAILABILITY

Think about what you have just done. You quickly looked over the information and located the section headed Senior Citizens. There you found what you were looking for.

What other information might your grandparents want?

Normal reading

On the other hand, if you are reading an article in a newspaper about last night's rock concert, you will want to know more than how much the tickets cost. You will want to know what songs the band performed, how the audience reacted to the new bass player and what the atmosphere at the concert was like. After you have finished reading the article, you will judge whether the writer thought the concert was a success or not. This second way of reading is *normal reading*. When you have finished reading you may decide to go and see the band when they are next in town.

Exercise

Band Report: Rebel Sound at the Town Hall

The five piece band *Rebel Sound* played to a packed Town Hall last night. They opened with the rock classic 'Hound Dog' and the new boy in the line-up, Dave Carter, provided a mean and moody bass to the band's raw and aggressive sound. Nicky White was in great form, singing better than I've ever heard him. What the audience really appreciated was that the *Rebels* sounded better live than they do on record. A rare event in the age of the synthesiser.

The *Rebels* played four driving tracks from their new album 'Alive and Well and Feelin' Good', and there was one outstanding number 'Searching for you in the Street' which, I'm happy to report, is to be their new single due in the shops next week.

The *Rebels* ended by responding to requests for the now famous 'Driving South' which somehow seems to get better every time I hear it.

I, for one, can't wait to see the *Rebels* again, and it was good to hear the band will be back on the road again later in the year. If you missed *Rebel Sound* this time make sure you make it to their next gig.

After normal reading you should be able to answer the following questions:

1 What overall impression do you get about *Rebel Sound's* performance?
2 What was so good about their performance?
3 When is their next single to be released?
4 What did the writer think of 'Driving South'?
5 What is the title of their new album?

Depth reading

Reading involves more than simply looking and recognising lines of words. Each word has a specific meaning and we often have to concentrate hard before we fully understand what point the writer is trying make. This does not mean that the writer has failed to put his point over clearly. He probably has. What we have to remember is that there are times when the points a writer is trying to make are difficult and take some effort to understand.

This is why reading is a skill which we have to go on improving. We have to concentrate when we read, and sometimes we have to struggle to understand before the meaning becomes clear. This way of reading is called *depth reading*. It is a method we often call upon to get us out of trouble, and it sometimes leads us into action.

Exercise These are letters written to a young worker by his training officer. The worker, Jim Baxter, is expecting a letter telling him that he will be attending the technical college on a day-release course. At work, the foreman hands Jim his letter. Jim reads it.

Hadley Electronics
Personnel Office
Hadley Works

19 August 19--

Mr James Henry
14 Holton Drive
Hadley H30 7BB

Our ref: RT/AWS

Dear Jim

After considerable discussions with your foreman it has been decided that you will not be attending the course at the technical college this year. This is no reflection on your ability, but other members of staff have priority over you. You will be included on the list being made up for the college for next year's course.

Thank you for showing interest in the course.

Yours sincerely

A Stonehouse

Andrew Stonehouse
Training officer

After reading the letter Jim was confused. He had been given a definite promise that he would be going to college. At first he couldn't understand it. He read the letter again and again. He went over every word. Then the penny dropped. He spotted something wrong.

Have you spotted it? Read through the letter carefully again until you do. Jim had received the wrong letter. Eventually the mix-up was sorted out. Once Jim had got *his* letter he read the text very carefully.

Dear Jim

This is to confirm that you will be attending Avondale Technical College on a day-release course, starting on Tuesday 23 September. College commences at 9 am and you are expected to be punctual.

Before going to college you will have to collect an attendance card from this office, and this card has to be signed by each one of your college lecturers. Failure to have this card signed and checked weekly by your training officer could mean a deduction from your wages.

You will be given a book allowance of £20 which should cover the cost of all the textbooks and stationery purchased for your college work. After you have bought these items bring them and the receipts to the office and you will be repaid.

At the end of your course you will sit three examinations and you are expected to pass these if you are to progress to the second year of the course. If you fail you may be allowed to sit the examinations again. This will depend on the reports we receive.

If you have any further queries do not hesitate to contact your training officer.

Yours sincerely

If you were Jim Baxter, what questions would you ask the training officer? Make a list of at least three penetrating questions.

Facts and opinions

When we are reading we have to remember that sometimes we will read facts and sometimes we will read opinions. We should know the difference between the two. If you read 'Christmas Day falls on the 25 December' you cannot dispute this statement. It is a *fact*. If you read that 'Christmas isn't as much fun as it used to be' you are reading someone's *opinion*.

We have to keep in mind that we are likely to come across opinions which we fully agree with. We should not think that because we see our view printed that somehow it must be a fact. Likewise, we must be willing to change our opinions when we are confronted with hard facts in our reading. It would be foolish simply to accept the facts and opinions which we tended to agree with.

Therefore, when we are reading we must be aware of the difference between facts and opinions. It would not be too much of an exaggeration to suggest that some writers tend to disguise their opinions as facts in order to influence us. Much propaganda is like this.

What are facts?

If you think that it is sometimes difficult to separate facts from opinions, it might come as no surprise that facts themselves are not what they seem. They can mislead us.

Read carefully the following letter sent to 'Grouse Corner':

> Dear Grouse Corner
>
> It is a fact, which we have to face up to, that today's young people are anti-marriage. It is also a fact that because of this we see the breakdown of decent behaviour in our country. Divorce is on the increase, there is violence on our streets, and young people are taking drugs and drinking vast quantities of alcohol. All because of the breakdown of family life.
>
> Harold Cross

If we accept that divorce is increasing, what are we to understand by this? What does this 'fact' actually mean? Does Mr Cross believe that young people are anti-marriage? How is this attitude linked with violence? Look at this graph of divorces and remarriages. What do you see?

Divorce and remarriage rates for women in Great Britain (shown as rate per thousand eligible women)

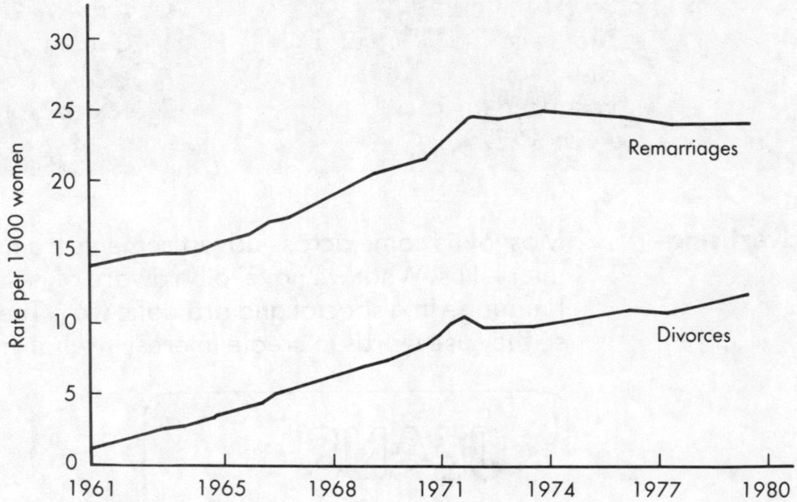

Note: In 1971 divorce was made easier by an Act of Parliament

Mr Cross is correct. Divorce is on the increase. But what about marriage? What do people do after they are divorced? Has family life really broken down?

When we read anything we should first concentrate on what we are reading, then fully understand what we have read. After we understand, we can then ask critical questions. You should be saying to yourself, 'I take the point but the writer should consider . . .'

Exercise Read through the review of the new album by *Rebel Sound* and draw up a list of the parts that are facts and those which are

Rebel Sound's latest album 'Alive and Well and Feelin' Good' is on the Rock Label (RORS 23798) and retails at £4.99, which is really great value when you consider the album contains 12 great tracks and you get exactly 42 minutes and 25 seconds of joy for your money from one of the best new bands in the UK. The album was produced and mixed by Duffy Grey whose last production was with the *Hunches*, and their album remained in the US Top 40 for 33 weeks and went Gold twice over. I think Grey will have the same success with *Rebel Sound*.

Of the 12 tracks, 9 are originals, and what is unusual for such a husky band is the use of strings on a closing track on Side One – a sweet one called 'Never Seen Anyone Like Her Before'. The really effective tracks are the rockers which the *Rebels* do best, and the album closes on Side Two with the incredible 'Searching for you in the Street'. I'd go so far as to say that this will become a rock classic to stand alongside the very best of the young Elvis Presley.

If I have a criticism of the album, it's with the playing of the new bass player Dave Carter. I don't think he sounded confident and I think he'll have to improve in his playing if he's not to become a passenger in one of the most exciting bands to come out of Liverpool since guess who. I can't say any more than that, can I?

opinion. Set out your lists following this example:

Facts	*Opinion*
1 Album called 'Alive and Well and Feelin' Good'.	**1** Great value.
2 Produced on Rock Label (RORS 23798).	**2** Joy for your money.

62 Advertising

Most of us come across advertisements from time to time which interest us. What we have to be aware of is that advertisers use language in a special and dramatic way. They want to impress us so they use words to create interest in what they are trying to sell.

> JEANS
>
> **BARGAIN PRICES**
>
> All the famous makes
> Most sizes — As new — Bargains
> Hurry while stocks last
> *This offer can never be repeated*
> Come along and see for yourself
>
> The Jean Corner
> High Street

Exercise

Look at the above advertisement. What are the *significant* words? What does the advertiser lead us to think?

There is an organisation which checks that advertising doesn't deliberately mislead us, but advertisements can fool us sometimes. This is what happened when Karen went to *The Jean Corner*.

Karen: I can't find any Mustang Jeans, size 10.
Assistant: We don't do them.
Karen: Oh!
Assistant: We've got some size 10 in Ranch Hand.
Karen: Yes, but the denim goes soft after you've washed them a couple of times.
Assistant: What about Cowgirl? They're a new line made in Hong Kong and they really are good value for money. Have a look.
Karen: They seem a bit dear.
Assistant: Yes, but there's three pounds off the manufacturer's recommended price.
Karen: Oh, I think I'll leave it. Thank you very much.

Karen's visit to *The Jean Corner* wasn't too successful. While the advertisement didn't set out to be dishonest, Karen took it at face value and didn't realise that the purpose of the advertisement was to get her to visit the shop. It is highly unlikely that she would have gone along if she had read:

> **JEANS**
>
> **EXPENSIVE**
>
> Names you have never heard of —
> Odd sizes — Slightly soiled
> Lose texture after washing
>
> Come along to
> The Jean Corner
> High Street

Emotional language

It may have struck you that what advertisers leave out is often more important than what they put in. They are not deliberately misleading us, but steering us away from the important information with the use of clever and exciting language. This emotive language costs a great deal of money—so it must be worth it from the advertiser's point of view. Here are some emotive words used in an advertisement published in a women's magazine:

> ✪ **Stallion** .... men stay cool
> ✪ **Stallion** .... men enjoy company
> ✪ **Stallion** .... men keep friends
> ✪ **Stallion** .... men make deals
> ✪ **Stallion** .... men score points
> ✪ **Stallion** .... men make happiness
> ✪ **Stallion** .... men bring joy
>
> Buy *Stallion* for *your* man before someone else does

In this advertisement the product is presented in a way that suggests that 'Stallion' men are successful and manly. It is the 'Stallion' men who make the deals and score the points. But there is a suggestion that *not* using this product may lead men to lose friends because of some slightly embarrassing reason which is *not* stated. 'Stallion-less' men are joyless and friendless because of their little 'problem' that we can't mention. As for the girls—well, their position is hopeless. Either they buy the product or lose their man!

Exercise Make a list of all the important items of information that have been left out of the 'Stallion' advert. What do you think is being advertised?

Brand names

The power of advertising is so great that when you read that the shop stocked jeans made by Mustang, Ranch Hand and Cowgirl you thought to yourself that you have never heard of these makes. Advertising is so powerful that the brand name itself can be more important than the item on sale! Sometimes the brand name actually replaces the original name of the item and becomes its common name. Can you think of a brand name that we now use instead of the word 'jeans'?

Exercise Look at this list of items and write down the brand names that come into your mind:

vacuum cleaner	expensive car
crisps	brown bread
chemist shop	children's interlocking plastic building bricks
scooter	power drill
large box of matches	malted bedtime drink
bicycle	paper handkerchiefs

Now compare your list with someone else's and see how many brand names appear twice.

Tips on reading

1. **Reading involves understanding. If you don't understand something go over it again.**
2. **Reading involves concentration. Don't think it's wrong if you have to read something more than once. Read it 10 times if necessary.**
3. **Don't be fooled by what you read.**
4. **Know the difference between fact and opinion.**
5. **Don't assume that what you read is true just because you agree with it.**
6. **Be critical when you read. Imagine you are with the writer and think of the questions you would like to ask him.**
7. **Read as often as you can. It doesn't matter what you read as long as you are getting something from it.**
8. **Never take advertisements at face value. Adverts that seem to be 'official' are often the most misleading. Take time and try to read 'between the lines'.**
9. **Always be suspicious of advertisements that ask for money through the post. Get hold of the product *before* you part with your money.**

On yer bike

You are cycling to work and the chain on your bike breaks and becomes entangled in the spokes of the back wheel. Not wishing to be late, you padlock your bike's back wheel and frame securely to the iron railings of a nearby park and walk to work. At lunchtime you return to find that the front wheel has been stolen, along with the tyre pump that you forgot to take with you.

From a local bike repair shop you get this estimate:

Estimate for repair of 'Kelver Easy Rider'
No 31EGH6574

	£
Renewal and replacement of badly worn chain	3.85
Straightening and realigning back wheel	2.35
Replacing broken spokes in back wheel	2.95
Fitting new front wheel	18.50
Replacement pump	1.70
	31.35

All prices include VAT

TASK

Fortunately, your bike is fully insured. First read through the schedule, and when you have read the questions thoroughly, answer all six questions in any order:

1 Am I entitled to claim anything from the insurers? Yes or No.

2 What repair costs will I be able to claim for? (Make a list of items)

3 What repairs can't I claim for? (Make a list of items)

4 Will I be able to claim my bus fares to work when my bike is out of use? Yes or No.

5 What compensation can I expect from the insurance company? (In cash)

6 Check the original estimate for accuracy. What should you do if there is an error? If necessary, correct any errors yourself before you begin these questions.

Home and leisure insurance
Schedule D — Pedal Cycle Cover — Conditions of Insurance

This section insures against loss of or damage to cycles whose description has been notified by the Insured to Underwriters, by fire, theft and/or accidental damage, including loss of or damage to tyres and accessories thereon by the same perils, provided such tyres and accessories are lost or damaged at the same time as the pedal cycle itself.

Limitations
Underwriters' liability shall not exceed the market value of the cycle at the time of the loss and shall in any case be limited to the sum insured specified in the Schedule and conditions.

Special exclusions
This section does not cover:

a any loss or damage caused by or through or in connection with any pedal cycle while such pedal cycle is being used for the purposes of any business other than by the Insured in person for his or her business or profession but excluding use for racing or pacemaking or time trials or for hire or reward or the carriage of goods in connection with any trade or business.

b loss of use, depreciation or damage caused by or resulting from wear and tear or breakdown.

c any loss or damage arising outside Great Britain, Republic of Ireland, Northern Ireland, Isle of Man or the Channel Islands.

d the first £2.50 of each and every claim.

Security
Compensation will be considered only if every insured cycle is securely padlocked at all times when left unattended.

Bournemouth

HOLIDAY FLATS AND FLATLETS

These premises listed below have received town planning approval or have established use rights to offer accommodation as described. The Corporation has no control over the standards of accommodation which may be offered as an alternative to those listed below

ADDRESS	TELEPHONE CC Corfe Castle, L Lyndhurst, R Ringwood, NM New Milton, H Highcliffe, A Andover, Ring 0202 unless otherwise indicated	House/Cottage/Maisonette	Flats – self-contained	Flats – non self-contained	Flatlets – self-contained	Flatlets – non self-contained	No of bathrooms/toilets non self-contained	Min/max occupants per unit	Minimum age of children – if any	WEEKLY TERMS pp = per person pu = per unit From £	To £
Jondel Seaside Holiday Flats, 13 St Johns Road, BH5 1EQ	20419	–	3	–	1	2	1/2	2/6	–	25.00	185.00 pu
Karen Court Holiday Flatlets, 9 Percy Road, BH5 1JF	36100	–	–	–	6	6	2/2	2/5	–	25.00	40.00 pp
Kensington Holiday Flats, 24 Hamilton Road, BH1 4EH	301230	–	2	–	–	2	1/1	2/7	–	20.00	pp
Kingfisher, 1207 Wimborne Road, BH10 7BW	514793	–	1	–	–	–	–	2/7	–	60.00	120.00 pu
Knole Dene, 26 Knole Road, BH1 4DH	708176	1	1	–	–	6	3/4	2/9	–	on application	
Knole Hall Holiday Flats, 60/64 Knyveton Road, BH1 3QX	301218	–	6	2		9	5/8	2/6	–	28.00	44.00 pp
Laguna Holiday Apartments, 16 Surrey Road, BH2 6AZ	767022	–	3	–	–	6	2/5	2/3	16	22.00	pp
Links View Holiday Flats, 506 Holdenhurst Road, BH8 9AJ	34293	–	3	–	–	–	–	2/5	–	58.00	148.50 pu
Longfleet House, 33 Longfleet Road, Poole	01-568 1788	–	6	–	–	–	–	2/10	–	50.00	140.00 pu
Longmoor, 23 Harvey Road	428669	–	3	–	–	–	–	2/6	–	15.00	25.00 pp
Lydiard House, 10 Chestnut Avenue, BH6 3SP	432894	–	–	3	–	–	1/1	2/4	–	48.00	70.00 pu
Lynmarie Holiday Flats, 17 Foxholes Road, BH6 3AT	429588	–	3	–	1	–	–	2/6	–	28.00	150.00 pu
Lynton Holiday Flats, 54 Westby Road	424075	–	4	–	2	2	2/2	1/8	–	35.00	255.00 pu
Lynwood Holiday Flats, 20 Stourcliffe Avenue, BH6 3PT	426299	–	3	–	–	–	–	2/7	–	25.00	168.00 pu
Lyttleton Lodge, 16 Florence Road, BH5 1HF	33503	–	10	–	1	5	2/3	1/8	–	20.00	286.00 pu
Mansfield House, 30 Florence Road	301478	–	6	1	–	–	–	2/6	–	37.00	180.00 pu
Marina Lodge, 27 Porchester Road. BH8 8JT	21163	–	–	–	2	6	2/3	2/4	2	25.00	pp
Marlborough Flats, 47b Parkwood Road, BH5 2BS	420533	–	2	–	–	–	–	2/6	5	25.00	35.00 pp
Merton Holiday Flats, 54 Christchurch Road, BH1 3PF	24080	–	14	3	–	–	3/3	2/6	–	25.30	51.75 pp
Meyrick Heights, 20 Meyrick Park Crescent, BH3 7AQ	20674	–	3	–	–	–	–	2/8	–	50.00	220.00 pu
Miami Court, 27a Surrey Road, BH4 9HW	764329	–	6	–	–	–	–	2/8	–	60.00	185.00 pu
Midchines Holiday Flats, 14 McKinley Road, BH4 8AQ	762974	–	7	–	–	–	–	2/8	–	30.00	200.00 pu
Midwood Holiday Flats, 64/66 Christchurch Road, BH1 3PF	33606	–	11	–	7	–	–	2/5	–	20.70	46.00 pp
Mills Holiday Flats and Flatlets, 7 Undercliff Road, BH5 1BL	731542	–	1	–	–	7	2/3	1/8	–	33.35	172.50 pu
Milton Court, 38 Milton Road, BH8 8LP	23148	–	2	–	–	3	2/2	2/4	–	25.00	40.00 pp
Minstrel Lodge Superior Hol Flats, 10 St Winifreds Rd , BH2 6NZ	25119	–	8	–	1	3	2/2	1/10	–	35.00	235.00 pu
Mondello Holiday Flatlets, 19 Stourcliffe Avenue, BH6 3PU	420174	–	–	–	–	3	1/1	1/2	12	30.00	pu
Montague House Holiday Flats, 1 Owls Road	37452/ 24823	–	5	–	–	–	–	2/8	–	60.00	230.00 pu
Moorside Court, 20 Madeira Road, BH1 1QG	23610	–	–	–	–	6	3/4	2/5	–	12.50	40.00 pp
Neville Court, 26a Derby Road	763943	–	3	–	–	–	–	2/6	–	60.00	210.00 pu
Norcliffe, 33 Grand Avenue, BH6 3SY	428919	–	2	–	–	4	1/2	2/6	6	30.00	160.00 pu
Norcroft House, 21 Norwich Avenue, BH2 5TG	24828	–	–	1	–	2	2/3	2/3	–	32.00	pu
Norfolk House Holiday Flats, 2 Walpole Road, BH1 4EN	37743	–	3	–	–	7	2/3	1/10	–	40.00	200.00 pu
Normanhurst, 36 Knole Road, BH1 4DH	34149	–	–	–	–	4	1/2	1/4	–	18.50	35.00 pp
Oak Lodge, 5 Browning Avenue, BH5 1NP	303562	1	1	–	–	–	–	4/6	–	45.00	125.00 pu
Ocean Court, 14 St Catherines Road, BH6 4AA	R 2013	–	6	–	–	–	–	2/7	–	25.00	270.00 pu
Ocean Court Holiday Apartments, 28 Derby Road, BH1 3QB	293186	–	28	–	–	–	–	2/6	–	64.40	281.75 pu
Oriel Lodge Holiday Flats, 4 Wollstonecraft Road, BH5 1JQ	34533	–	3	2	–	–	1/1	2/7	–	45.00	pu
Osbourne House, 22 Porchester Road, BH8 8JY	21504	–	1	–	–	3	1/2	2/4	–	18.00	pp
Overcliffe Mansions, 1/3 Manor Road, BH1 3HA	764450	–	7	–	–	–	–	2/6	4	on application	
Owls Court, 14 Owls Road, BH5 1AF	35377	–	–	–	–	10	1/3	2/4	–	25.00	pp
Oxford Luxury Holiday Apartments, 6 Lansdowne Road BH1 1SD	22654/ 26662	–	3	–	2	–	–	1/6	5	40.00	300.00 pu
Palm Lodge, 2 Watkin Road, BH5 1HP	35504	–	–	–	–	6	2/3	2/4	–	20.00	36.00 pp
Park Mount, 5 Meyrick Park Crescent, BH3 7AG	24666	–	–	3	–	5	3/4	2/4	–	19.00	32.00 pp

TASK

You, your two friends and a dog decide to book a flat for a week's holiday in Bournemouth during the first week in August. You estimate that altogether you will have a maximum of about £400, which of course must include an allowance for spending money, food, and petrol for your friend's car.

Look at the list of flats and flatlets available, and select suitable accommodation for your holiday. You can assume that you will be asked to pay the maximum weekly terms. You will have completed this task when you have:

a made a list estimating all your holiday expenses

b written a short letter asking for more details about the accommodation and requesting a booking form

Explorer packages

1. You want to buy a Yorkshire Railtourer ticket. You plan to use your ticket during the August Bank Holiday. Is this possible?
2. You plan to spend six days of your holiday exploring the region. Would it be cheaper to buy your tickets on a daily basis or to buy a Railtourer ticket? What is the difference in price?

Yorkshire explorer packages

There are more places to visit by bus than you ever thought! This document indicates the range of day trips which you can make on Yorkshire bus routes starting from Leeds, Bradford or Harrogate.

Explorer packages have been put together to enable you to enjoy a day out in the countryside or to visit some of the many attractions detailed in this document at a special low price.

Every trip is different but every price is the same with reduced rates for children and old age pensioners and special rates for families.

Adult	£2.00
Child	£1.00
OAP	£1.50
Family (up to 2 adults and 2 children)	£4.00

All give you one day's travel – on the date of your choice – following an explorer route. Buy your *Day Explorer* tickets in advance at local bus company offices or Tourist Information Centres.

Yorkshire Railtourer Ticket. This ticket is on sale from 2 May to 2 October. It allows 7 consecutive days unlimited travel commencing at or after 0900 Monday to Friday, any train on Saturdays, Sundays and Bank Holidays within the area bounded by the following stations: York, Selby, Malton, Thirsk, Northalterton, Huddersfield, Sheffield, Doncaster, Worksop, East Retford, Gainsborough, Thorne and Goole.

Second class only – Adult £10.00, Child £5.00

The bad driver's code

68 A penalty points system for motoring offences now means that drivers have a clearer understanding about offences which lead to a driving disqualification. If a driver receives 12 points within a 3-year period he will be liable to disqualification. Here is the code:

Offence	Points
Reckless driving	10
Careless or inconsiderate driving	2–5
Being in charge of a motor vehicle when unfit through drink or drugs	10
Being in charge of a motor vehicle with alcohol above prescribed limit	10
Failing to provide a specimen for a breath test	4
Failing to provide specimen for analysis (in 'in charge' cases)	10
Carrying passenger on motor cycle illegally (eg sidesaddle)	1
Failing to comply with traffic directions	3
Leaving vehicle in dangerous position	3
Failing to stop after accident	5–9
Failing to give particulars or report an accident	4–9
Contravention of construction and use regulations	3
Driving without licence	2
Failing to comply with conditions of licence	2
Driving with uncorrected defective eyesight	2
Refusing to submit to test of eyesight	2
Driving while disqualified as under age	2
Driving while disqualified by order of court	6
Using, or causing or permitting use of, motor vehicle uninsured and unsecured against third party risks	4–8
Contravention of traffic regulations on special roads (eg motorways)	3
Contravention of pedestrian crossing regulations	3
Failure to obey sign exhibited by school crossing patrol	3
Contravention of order prohibiting or restricting use of street playground by vehicles	2
Exceeding a speed limit	3
Taking or attempting to take a vehicle without consent or lawful authority or driving or attempting to drive a motor vehicle so taken or allowing oneself to be carried in a motor vehicle so taken	8
Going equipped for stealing with reference to theft or taking of motor vehicle	8
Stealing or attempting to steal a motor vehicle	8

A leading Department of Transport official said that this method is fairer for drivers and easier for the courts: 'This is a major step forward in dealing with repeated offenders and courts in all parts of the country will now have the same yardstick to help distinguish between major offences and those which are less serious.' The official also made the point that the new system is a lot simpler to understand.

It was the Government's intention that all offences should carry a fixed number of points, but strong pressure from the

Royal Automobile Club has meant that certain types of offence now carry a range of points to be imposed at the discretion of the courts.

Drivers who break the law should now be able to agree that their offences are graded according to their relative seriousness. Purely technical offences, though they still merit penalty points, earn fewer of them. Justice will now be seen to be done.

One interesting feature is that 'being in charge of a motor vehicle when unfit through drink or drugs' and 'being in charge when over the prescribed limit' carry only 10 points and so no automatic disqualification. The courts now look a little more leniently upon the driver who sleeps if off on the back seat instead of driving the vehicle. Drunk drivers are automatically banned.

Anyone convicted of more than one offence committed on the same occasion will incur the highest number of points awarded for one of the offences. And the 3-year period is measured on each occasion backwards from the date when the latest offence was committed.

When the licence is issued to drivers after a period of disqualification it will be 'wiped clean' in that none of the previously incurred points will be recorded on it. However, the licence will refer to any disqualification imposed during the previous 4 years, or 11 years if alcohol or drugs driving offences were involved.

TASK

Answer all questions

1. Explain the circumstances that would lead a driver to be disqualified from driving.
2. In your own words explain the main advantages of this totting-up method of penalties.
3. How many points would a driver without a licence 'score' if he is caught exceeding the speed limit?
4. Can you think of any driving offences that are not awarded penalty points?
5. What is the difference between being in charge of a vehicle when drunk and driving when drunk? What penalty points would the court award in each case?
6. Can you identify any flaws or disadvantages in this coding system?

Passive smoking

What is passive smoking?

Passive smoking is breathing air which contains other people's tobacco smoke. Tobacco smoke is a serious cause of indoor air pollution. Two cigarettes smoked in a closed room can give as much as 20 times more air pollution than is found in city centre streets.

Only two out of every five adults smoke cigarettes. But nearly everyone is at times a passive smoker. Most non-smokers find it very unpleasant to be in a smoky room, and about 50% say they sometimes suffer from sore nose or throat, smarting eyes, coughs, dizziness or headaches caused by others' cigarette smoke. Some people get more serious symptoms.

A cigarette produces two kinds of cigarette smoke:

Roughly 75% of the smoke from a lit cigarette goes straight out into the air as **sidestream smoke**. The smoker inhales the remaining 25% as **mainstream smoke**, and breathes half of this out again. In total, 85-90% of cigarette smoke gets into the air which others breathe.

The smoker / The passive smoker

Effects on adults

Nicotine, carbon monoxide and other chemicals from a burning cigarette are present in the blood stream of a passive smoker. A non-smoker in a smoky room may breathe in the equivalent of one cigarette for every 20 being smoked in the same room.

Effects on babies

Passive smoking begins in the womb. Pregnant women who smoke are more likely to have small babies, and small babies are more likely to die at birth or shortly afterwards. Pregnant women shouldn't smoke, but neither should fathers-to-be, because the sidestream smoke from their cigarettes may be breathed in by the mother and affect the baby.

Would-be-fathers are also warned that smoking can affect fertility. Results of work done on a group of men in an Edinburgh infertility clinic showed that smokers produced higher numbers of abnormal sperm than non-smokers.

Effects on children

Babies run twice the risk of developing a serious chest illness if both parents smoke. The children of parents who smoke are twice as likely to suffer from colds, coughs, phlegm, and, more seriously, pneumonia, bronchitis and tonsillitis, than children of non-smokers. Smokers' children also grow up with less healthy lungs, and have more days off sick from school. Parents who smoke set a bad example, and their children are more likely to start smoking than are children of non-smokers.

TASK

1. Explain in your own words the meaning of 'passive smoking'.
2. What is the difference between 'mainstream' and 'sidestream' smoke?
3. Why does sidestream smoke contain higher concentrations of poisonous chemicals than mainstream smoke?
4. How is it that babies in the womb can be affected by cigarette smoke? (You will have to think about this.)
5. Make a list of all the diseases that are associated with tobacco smoke.
6. Select *one* of the dangers of passive smoking and produce a small poster on A4, designed to inform and warn the public. Maximum visual impact is essential.

Death is a two-wheeled dream

by *Frank Connolly*

'The thing is,' a young biker told me outside the Slade Café, 'you forget that young people like the danger of ridin' their machines. I mean there's nothing like having a burn-up—nothing like it in this world.'

Maybe. But the 1200 dead and 22 000 seriously injured in 1980 make grim statistical reading. At the end of the same year there were 1.4 million motor bikes. That's 7 per cent of all the motor vehicles on the road. But harsh statistics come to light when we consider that just under a fifth of all road deaths and a quarter of serious injuries in 1980 involved motor cycles.

A research worker who specialises in aspects of road behaviour told me: 'It really is frightening when you think that one person will die for every 841 bikes on the road. Now those are alarming figures.'

When we think of the concern given to other aspects of young people's behaviour the research worker is amazed that these figures don't lead to a public outcry. 'We all know that young people are attracted to bikes. They can afford them and the manufacturers are very conscious of the appeal of bikes, especially to the young male. Hence the big emphasis on getting the image right when designing a bike. But an 18-year-old is 6 times more likely to be killed or hurt than a motor cyclist in his 50s.'

What can be done to reduce this carnage on our roads and the terrible waste of young lives?

The Department of Transport has introduced more stringent tests for learner riders. There is a *Part One* test which is aimed to test a rider's skill at negotiating corners. This test also checks to see how much the learner knows about safe riding techniques. *Part Two* is taken on the road and if passed the rider can leave his L plates at home, take on passengers, and ride a bigger and more powerful machine.

However, there are people who think that even this training is inadequate. One senior doctor put it this way. 'What I would like to see is far more emphasis on actually preventing accidents. We want an all-out preventive approach, and that includes thinking about bike design and also about the roads the machines are driven on. It would cost more money, but after spending the last 10 years in a casualty unit I can assure you it would be money well spent.'

It does seem strange, to say the least, that given the 'statistics of death and injury' the motor cycle can still be taken straight onto the road by the most inexperienced of riders. All you need to do is buy a licence.

At the Walton Cycle Club I met one biker who, on his own admission, was 'a bit of a nutter' in his younger days. He was speaking out of experience when he told me: 'When you're young you don't really want people telling you what to do all the time. That's where a lot of these official training places go wrong. With the best will in the world some of the instructors just don't talk the same language as the bikers. That's where places like this can help, and organisations like the Motor Cycle Association. Here we're on the same wavelength as the youngsters and I think we can get the message through to them.'

The message from this Club and others like it is on defensive riding. Riders should always be on the lookout for danger. The Royal Society for the Prevention of Accidents has also promoted campaigns like the 'Think Bike' series of ads on TV.

Whatever the message, one thing should be clear. Something has to be done to reduce this tragic loss of life and serious injury on our roads. *The statistics of death are a national scandal.*

TASK

Read the preceding article two or three times and with the help of a dictionary answer the following questions:

1. What was the total number of people killed and seriously injured in motor cycle accidents in 1980?
2. Estimate the total number killed in all road accidents in the same year.
3. In your own words, explain the following terms as used in the article:
   - *a* having a burn-up
   - *b* conscious of the appeal of bikes
   - *c* harsh statistics
   - *d* getting the image right
   - *e* stringent tests
   - *f* on the same wavelength
   - *g* defensive riding.
4. Explain the basic difference between *Part One* and *Part Two* of the test for learner riders.
5. Make a list of all the suggestions put forward in the article to further improve motor cycle safety.
6. What suggestion(s) would *you* make to improve safety?
7. What kind of customers would you say used Slade Café? Guess why it has this name (or) suggest another suitable name for a café used by bikers?

Display ads

74

A new British motor-bike is about to be launched. These two advertisements have been prepared by the makers for publication in the UK.

A

THE TORNADO 249

The TORNADO 249 is a new concept in bike design. Fashioned out of raw steel to cope with the most savage weather conditions and big-man handling, this dream-machine offers today's bikers tomorrow's ideas in bike design. Jet-black tank and frame with steel blue trimmings, wind-cheating aerodynamics, big-sound powerful engine with slick transmission, four-score speed, fog-cutting lamps, and the latest electrics.
Test ride the Tornado 249 and see if you can resist!

B

THE TORNADO 249

For the connoisseur biker

Specifications

Engine:	Air-cooled single overhead cam single operating four valves. Capacity 249 cc Wet sump lubrication.
Transmission:	Seven-speed with internal gear ratios from 2.307 in first to 0.838 in seventh
Electrics:	12-volt 3-amp battery charged by alternator. Head beam 30/35 watts.
Dimensions:	Length 95 ins, 35 in wide, height 45 in Weight 279 lb.

Ask your dealer for a test ride

TASK

1. The advertisers wish to place one of these advertisements in each of the following publications. Which advertisement is suitable for which publication? Give reasons for your choice:

   Motor Cycle News
   New Musical Express
   The Sun newspaper
   A road transport magazine

2. Which of the two advertisements uses words to appeal to the emotions? Make a list of words and phrases that are supposed to excite the reader.

3. As an experiment, the manufacturers of the Tornado 249 decide to extend their advertising campaign into the car-user market. They believe that many car drivers find motoring too expensive and might be persuaded to change from four wheels to two.

   Using the existing advertisements as a guide, prepare a new advertisement for publication in a motoring weekly magazine aimed at the car driver who is getting fed up with the high cost of motoring.

Slogans

TASK

1 Slogans or catch-phrases are often used by advertisers to 'grab' our attention. Some slogans, especially those to which we are constantly exposed, become so familiar that we have difficulty ignoring them. To what products do you associate these slogans?

Gotta lot of bottle
Sch . . . you know who
Sign of the Black Horse
Simply years ahead
Flexible friend
Full of Eastern promise
Sign of the oak tree
The Australian for lager
Everyone's a fruit and nut case
Cleans floors fast
A major contribution to road safety
Join the Professionals
We'll take more care of you
All because the lady loves
The bank that likes to say yes
The alcohol free lager

2 Invent suitable advertising slogans for these new products:

- *The 'Tornado 249'*—a new British motor bike
- *'Coldwash'*—a powder detergent for cold-water washing
- *'Stallion'*—a splash-on lotion for men

3 A new technology company has been established to manufacture goods for the British market. They plan to market two products:

- Computer toys and games for children
- A robot machine for automated factory production

Invent original brand names and attractive advertising slogans for both product ranges.

7 Writing clearly

If anyone tells you that writing comes easily to them, you can be sure that they are either a genius or what they write is not worth reading. Writing clearly and well is *difficult*. It requires a lot of hard work and plenty of practice. Some famous authors might spend a whole day writing 750 words before they are satisfied!

Why then is writing so difficult? One of the main reasons is that a writer is not in face-to-face contact with his reader. The reader must understand what has been written without the personal help of the writer. For example, if someone says something you cannot understand, you can ask the person to repeat it or to explain it another way. It is not possible to do this as a reader. Therefore, if you are writing to someone, you must make sure that what you write can be understood.

Imagine that you are having mechanical trouble with, say, your motor bike. You take it to the garage and the mechanic asks you to explain the problem. Then imagine that instead of going to the garage personally you have to write to them giving a detailed explanation of the mechanical faults. Which of the two methods is the easier?

The secret of clear writing

So what is the secret of clear writing? The secret is that there is no secret. Writing, for the most part, is like any other skill: it has to be learnt and then practised until it comes out the way it should. It is really no different from learning the guitar because you want to become a rock musician; the hard work comes first, the glory later.

At the top of page 77 is a real-life example of a school leaver applying for a job as an apprentice mechanic in a local garage. He has been asked to write a statement about why the job should be given to him. You don't have to be clever to guess that Pete never got the job. He wasn't even considered for an interview. The garage manager probably thought that if a young person does not take enough care to write a decent statement then he might not take the trouble to be a careful mechanic. Yet the manager may be wrong about this. Just because Pete writes badly does not automatically mean that he will be a bad mechanic. Nevertheless,

My Dad told me to write for this job becaus he thinks Im a great mechanick when I strip down at the weekend. Im working on an old car and he lets me use his gears. And then there is my job as a paper-boy. Im good at that as well, Im never late or anything. If you want me to go to colledge I dont mind – I have a couple of mates who go and I can go with them, as long as I get paid. By the way I have some CSEs that might be OK for this work. If you give me a chance I will be a freind for life. Cheers.

Pete

Pete did not get an interview mainly because he failed to understand that people make important decisions about us because of the way we write.

Let us help Pete to improve upon his original statement:

I believe that I am well suited for this job. I have always been interested in engines and cars and I spend a lot of time at home at the weekends stripping down an old car and putting it together again. My father is a qualified car mechanic and he gives me plenty of advice and lends me his tools. I have CSE qualifications in technical drawing and metalwork which should help me as an apprentice mechanic.

If I get this job I promise to work hard and do what is expected of me. I am keen to learn about the garage trade and I am looking forward to attending college for extra instruction. I also think that reliability and punctuality are important and I have a good record in my part-time job as a paper-boy.

Peter Day

You can see that this second statement is a great improvement. It is written clearly and goes straight to the point in the first sentence. It brings out the important facts that Peter:

- is keen to get the job
- knows something about engines
- has suitable qualifications and is keen to get more
- has had work experience
- thinks working hard, punctuality and reliability are important

Two rules of clear writing

The first rule about clear writing is that we should always try to **plan** what we are going to write. Jotting down our ideas and then arranging them in logical order is the first step. Then we can group similar ideas into sections, each section may eventually become a paragraph. In the second statement you can see that the first paragraph deals with Pete's knowledge of mechanics and the second paragraph with his attitudes towards working.

The second rule is that we should always keep in mind the kind of person we are writing to. We must remember to use the correct **style** of writing. The style we use in a letter to a works manager should be different from that to a close friend. In the first statement, Pete is far too casual when he ends his statement with the words: 'I will be a friend for life. Cheers.' This is not the style to use when writing to a future employer.

Exercise

Now try this for yourself. On page 79 is part of a letter written by a teenage girl living in Birmingham to her girlfriend in London. She is making travel arrangements, and describing her experiences at the *Status Quo* concert at the NEC (National Exhibition Centre).

If you read this extract carefully you will notice that the details about travelling have been mixed in with the writer's adventures at the *Status Quo* concert—so much so that it is difficult to understand exactly what travelling arrangements have been made.

To complete this exercise extract all the information about the travelling arrangements and rewrite it in one paragraph to make more sense. Make a list of all the other mistakes in the original extract.

Punctuation

Punctuation is necessary because without it we cannot write in a way that makes sense to the reader. When we speak, for example, we can change the tone or volume of our voice so that the listener can tell whether we are sad or angry.

When are you coming to see me? I'll meet you at New street
Station in Brum. You should have come with me to see Quo
at the NEC - _fabuloso_ - the sound were terific - You should
have heard Ricki sing your favorite song - _fantastic_ - I
can't believe he is so old!!! - he had a big white hat and
Washed-out jeans - _incredible_!!! If you get the early train I
can meet you on platform 7. We can have a cofee or
something at the station before we go into town - talking
about cofee - guess who I met at the Quo concert - Lloyd Taylor -
you remember, he is the guy who won that Disco Crazy
competition. I saw Prince Charles as well - I nearly touched
him - WOW!!! (short for _Way Out Woyalty_) Later we went
for a cofee - don't worry, nothing developed - but what a
great mover he is!!! See you on Sat then. And I mean on
the 13th of the month - don't come on the rong Sat like
last time! I expect the train will get in about 11. And bring
some money with you this time - after that concert I'm
broke.

Since it is not possible to do this when writing, we have to use punctuation to recreate the illusion of speech on paper so the reader can understand us. What would writing look like without punctuation? Here is an extract from a space fantasy with the punctuation removed:

> pop pop crack hammond guided his freighter through the exploding space mines sabrina had sown them cleverly but hammond was an alpha one pilot and he was determined to outwit her zoom crack krump glorious yellow orange flames lit his cockpit as the mines detonated hammonds taut brain flashed an image of sabrina at their first meeting on galantia ii what a contrast then she was a young pilot uncorrupted by that space germ bantum why why did it have to happen it was hammonds last thought a sabrina special exploded a metre from his head and hammond and his freighter joined the galactic debris the space witch had claimed another hero

Although the extract is possible to understand, it is not easy, and may take a second reading. We cannot expect our reader to suffer as much as this!

Yet this is the way we would write if we reproduced our voices in writing. When we speak, we don't use commas, full stops, question marks, paragraphs, etc; we use our voices naturally in a way that is understandable to the listener. So punctuation is a vital tool in transforming speech into writing.

When we include the punctuation, the passage comes to life:

> Pop! Pop! Crack!
>
> Hammond guided his freighter through the exploding space mines. Sabrina had sown them cleverly, but Hammond was an Alpha-one pilot and he was determined to outwit her.
>
> Zoom! Crack! Krump! Glorious yellow-orange flames lit his cockpit as the mines detonated. Hammond's taut brain flashed an image of Sabrina at their first meeting on Galantia II. What a contrast! Then she was a young pilot, uncorrupted by that space-germ Bantum. Why? Why did it have to happen?
>
> It was Hammond's last thought. A Sabrina special exploded a metre from his head and Hammond and his freighter joined the galactic debris. The space-witch had claimed another 'hero'.

First, look at the way the passage has been divided into paragraphs, each paragraph dealing with a slightly different topic. Then see the way each paragraph has been split up into sentences, each sentence complete in itself dealing with a separate idea within the topic (study the last three sentences).

Punctuation marks

The two basic punctuation marks are the full stop and the comma. Although there are other important marks such as colons and semi-colons (: ;), inverted commas (' '), apostrophes ('s), question and exclamation marks (? !), etc, if you can use full stops and commas effectively you will improve your basic writing skills.

The full stop

The main use of a full stop is to end a sentence. People who have trouble writing clearly usually find it difficult to know when a sentence ends. Here is an example:

> Some young people smoke to impress their friends, they hate being told they are stupid by the older generation.

It is fairly easy to see that there are two separate ideas in this sentence which would be better kept apart—why some young people smoke and what they hate. It should be written in two sentences:

> Some young people smoke to impress their friends. They hate being told they are stupid by the older generation.

If you have problems knowing when to use full stops and when to begin new sentences it is usually safer to keep sentences fairly short.

Exercise

Rewrite the following in three sentences. You may change the wording slightly if you wish:

> Some people start smoking when they are at junior school although many older people have given up smoking in the last ten years, except young working women, whose cigarette consumption may be increasing, are causing some concern with the medical profession.

The comma

Commas are more difficult to handle than full stops. They can be used to separate words or phrases in a list:

> The scene of the accident was strewn with the shattered safety glass of windscreens, twisted metal, an odd shoe, a pair of glassless spectacles, and a child's doll with a broken head.

They can also be used as a method of introducing additional information inside a sentence. Here is a complete sentence:

> My brother is unemployed.

Using commas we can expand to:

> My brother, who is a qualified mechanic, is unemployed.

Exercise

Rewrite the following passage putting in the six missing commas:

> The detective leaning on the back of his chair looked at the stolen goods spread on the table. There were two engagement rings a gold watch a bundle of hand written letters some old coins and a small silver brooch with a platinum cross.

Repeat words

When you write or speak do you tend to repeat certain favourite words like 'nice' or 'great' or 'boring'?

Although it is sometimes convenient for us to use the same word more than once, to the reader or to the listener it can become

We've bought a great little house next door to the Taylor's—you know, those nice people we met on that great little holiday last year. We have a great big garden full of nice flowers. It would be great if you could visit us sometime next year.

monotonous. Above is part of a letter written by someone who has recently moved house:

Exercise Rewrite the above extract in a more interesting way.

Tips about clear writing

1. **Before you write anything, always *think* first about what it is you want to say and the kind of person you are writing to or for.**
2. **Jot down any ideas that come into your mind (they may be key words, main points, arguments you wish to use, etc) roughly on paper.**
3. **Sort out your ideas in some sort of logical order and keep adding new ideas as you go along.**
4. **When you are ready to begin you should think about dividing your ideas into paragraphs, if these are required.**
5. **If in doubt, use short sentences. Avoid using too many dashes—it is lazy writing.**
6. **Write a complete rough copy first and read it carefully. This is the time to be critical of yourself. Check spellings in a dictionary.**
7. **Check punctuation and be ruthless in cutting out slang words, especially in important documents.**
8. **Show your rough copy to another person and ask for any opinions and suggestions—two brains are better than one.**
9. **When you are satisfied that the rough copy is satisfactory, write the finished copy neatly.**
10. **Read over what you have written.**

First-aid

TASK

The following sentences and headings are mixed up. Without moving sentences out of their group, rearrange and rewrite them in three separate paragraphs, each with its own heading. You may add or change words if you wish, as long as the basic facts remain. Begin the exercise by working out the correct sequence of sentences in Group 1.

Group 1—First-aid for cuts

- Cover the burn with a clean, non-fluffy cloth like a cotton pillow-case or linen tea-towel.
- It is important to do this for at least ten minutes to reduce the heat in the skin.
- Do not put butter, oil or ointment on a burn.
- If burnt clothes are stuck to the skin, don't try to take them off.
- Immediately put the burn under cold water, or run plenty of cold water over it.
- Do not prick any blisters because you will let germs in.
- If the burn is serious seek medical attention.
- This cuts down the danger of infection.
- Take off anything tight like a belt or jewellery because burnt skin can swell.

Group 2—First-aid for burns

- Put some padding between the legs.
- This is especially important if you think the injury is to the neck or spine.
- Do not move the injured person unless the person is still in a dangerous place.
- If it is the arm that is injured and it can be moved, gently put it in a sling or support.
- If it is a leg that is broken, tie it gently but firmly to the uninjured leg before moving.
- Try to get help before attempting to move an injured person.
- If the injured person must be moved, be very gentle to avoid further damage.
- Do not offer food or drink.

Group 3—First-aid for broken bones

- Do not do this if you think the limb is broken.
- This may take 10 minutes or more.
- Keep pressing until the bleeding stops.
- Do not offer drinks after an accident if you think an anesthetic may be used later.
- Don't use a tourniquet or tie anything so tightly that it stops the circulation.
- If a limb is cut, lie down and raise the injured limb to help reduce bleeding.
- If there is severe bleeding, press firmly on the wound using a pad of clean cloth if available, or your fingers.
- If the wound is dirty, or the accident happened outside, ask your doctor about a tetanus injection.
- Cover the wound with a clean dressing.
- If it is a large wound, try to press the edges of the wound together.

Punctuation

TASK

Using the space fantasy exercise as a guide, punctuate the following extract. First read it a few times and decide how it should be divided into paragraphs.

detective george hanratty glared at the prisoner maloney reminded him of a reptile he once kept as a child he had a small pointed head beady sore eyes a rough bubbly skin and a protruding tongue that darted and withdrew rapidly as he lied the words mother were tattooed across both knuckles the detective hated him beyond words maloney could hear himself talking it wasnt the first time he had been up against hanratty five years earlier hanratty had been a constable in c division maloney trapped in a dark alley had given the young constable a bad time he told the jury it was mistaken identity and they believed him he had a feeling that this time would be different ring ring the phone burst into life hanrattys wife was expecting him home for supper she always expected him home on time she couldnt get used to the idea she was a coppers wife how many times had he let her down who knows she didnt care anymore maloney was lying through his teeth hanratty wondered how long it would be before he was due to retire how many more creeps like maloney would he have to interview he thought of five thousand five thousand dead beats he could see them lined up but he couldnt see the end of the line

Why I want this job

TASK

You are applying for a job you have always wanted. On the application form there is a large space under the heading 'Why I want this job'.

In 125–50 words explain to the employer all the reasons why he should give you the job.

Danger!

TASK

Look at these illustrations closely. They show everyday dangers to be found in and outside the home. The first completed example gives sensible advice to the average householder about the dangers of pills and medicines to children.

To complete this task:

- compose a suitable heading or title
- write one or two short paragraphs giving sensible advice to the average family. If you wish, you may expand your advice to include further guidance of a helpful kind *beyond* what is illustrated (like the advice about visiting other people's homes in the first example).

1

Pills and medicines

Keep medicines out of children's reach. Use a cupboard that locks, and keep it locked. Keep all your pills and medicines in the cupboard. Don't be tempted to keep the odd bottle out just for convenience.

Be especially careful when your child goes to visit grandparents or other people's houses, or when a grandparent or friend comes to stay. A lot of people still have dangerous medicines in easy-to-open bottles and they forget to keep them away from children.

2

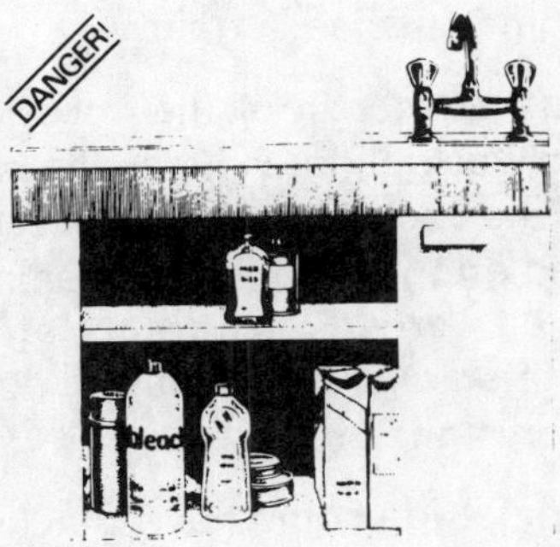

3

4

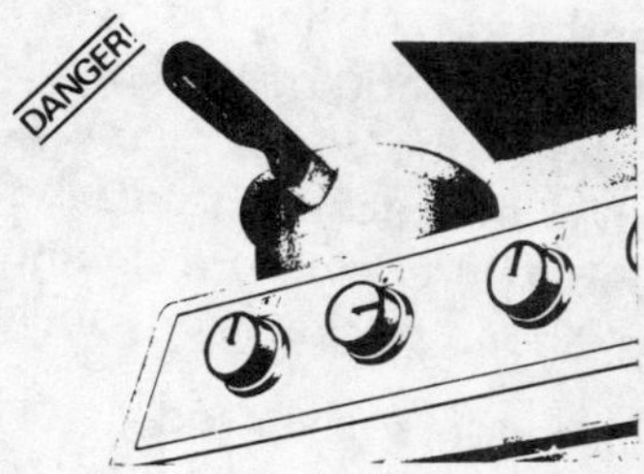

5

6

7

8

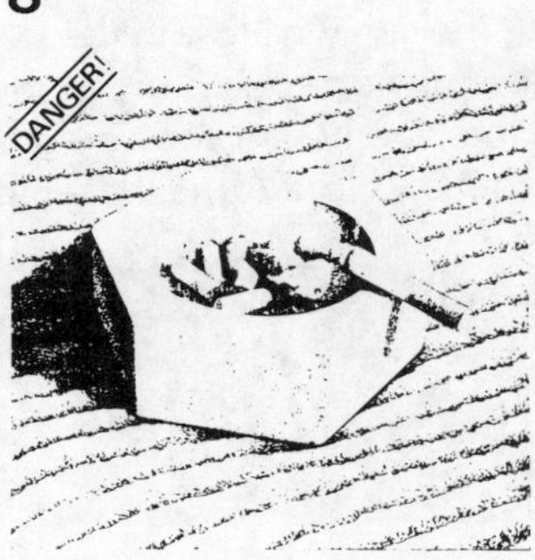

9

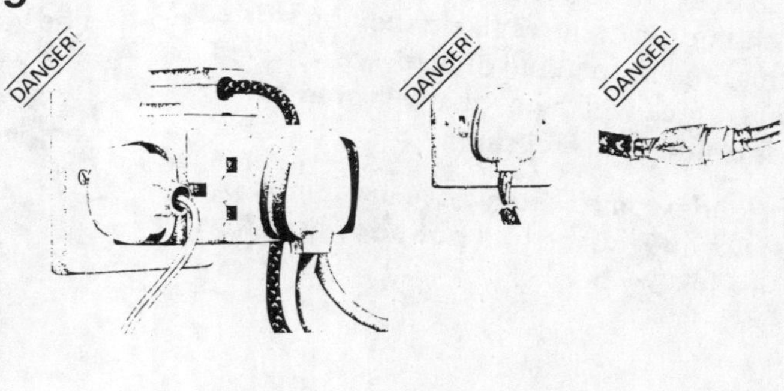

I like your style

News from the green table

Last Sunday night saw a thrilling climax to the Hilton Snooker Tournament. After four **frames** honours were shared between the two **masters**, Wells and Henderson. At the start of the fifth frame, Wells, who had been **clinical** all evening, **broke** for the **decider**. How he must have felt as he watched the **cue-ball kiss** a couple of reds before **sinking** into the top right hand **pocket** is anyone's guess.

But Henderson sensed victory. After **stalking** the stable he went on to make a **break** of 42 before **miscueing** on a red which was placed invitingly over the middle pocket. But it didn't matter. Wells sensationally miscued his next shot and became terribly **iffy**. When Henderson moved to the table Wells seemed to be punishing his cue by vigorously **chalking it**. Here was a man in trouble.

Henderson then went on to make another break, this time setting a competition record of 97 before wildly **slashing** at a **safe shot**. But the night was his. Wells tried to come back with an ambitious **snooker** which failed and opened the table for Henderson. A champion of the **rest**, Henderson started his final break until all that was left was the black which he took with **stun and left side off the cushion**.

Henderson raised his cue in triumph, knowing that he had **potted** himself into the history books.

Cricket, lovely cricket

Nothing can beat spending a Sunday watching someone **winging** a ball in the hope that it beats his opponent or at least forces him into making a false shot. Cricket, at its club best, can still create an exciting atmosphere and make up for many a dreary English summer.

Yesterday at the Pavilion Ground we had everything you could possibly want from a cricket match and there was no real disappointment at the end, even though the game finished in a draw.

The fast bowlers took their **prey** and the crowd was delighted when the **middle order** men **collapsed** to a succession of wicked **googlies**. Hilton's opening batsmen were **taken at short leg** and in this **limited over match** this all added up to a very tight finish.

The home side could have clinched it but they hadn't any answers to the questions Hawkins was asking as he **took command at the crease**. However, after a fine showing he went two short of his **half century** to the third **delivery** of the day from Cowens. This was a good one which straightened on **pitching**, knocking back the **off-stump**. For someone so late in the day he had Swan **leg-before** and with the second of his third **over** he had Murray **caught behind** by Williams.

By the time the umpires **pulled stumps** it was a little after seven and at this time of the year the sun was low in the sky. As the well-satisfied spectators made their way to the club house you could taste the enjoyment of a late August evening.

'Wicketkeeper'

These two articles have been written in a style suitable for a particular kind of readership. The writers have 'tuned in' to their specialist readers by using key words which have been picked out in bold type.

TASK

Write a similar article of about 150 words on a subject or an interest that you know about. When you have finished you should be able to underline at least eight different key words or phrases.

At the end of the article briefly explain in simple English the meanings of your key words.

Litter

To all litter louts

Have you noticed all the rubbish lying about the factory? This won't do, you know. I'm not having people throw their fag packets and sandwich papers on the floor of this factory. You wouldn't do it in your own homes and you're not doing it here. Besides anything else it is very dangerous and can lead to accidents. If things do not improve I will have to see the manager about what to do about it. He might ask you to take a wage cut to pay for a cleaner. Anyway please put your rubbish in the proper place. Thanks.

Ron Green
Foreman

TASK

This notice was found pinned to a factory wall. The foreman is concerned about the increase in litter. Do you think the notice is badly written? Would you be offended by it?

Show the foreman how you would have written it. It needs to be completely rewritten.

The Tall Story Club

88

A gathering of eminent tall story tellers had to be cancelled after a chapter of accidents struck down several of the participants.

One was unable to attend because of severe lacerations to his thighs and a broken leg. He telephoned the meeting from a Midlands hospital to say he had acquired these injuries as a result of a prank by schoolchildren, but seemed reluctant to explain further.

Our enquiries have revealed that the professor went into a public convenience in Nottingham where vandals had spread superglue on the seats. The professor, finding himself stuck fast, banged fruitlessly on the door for more than an hour before anyone came to his rescue.

Eventually, an attendant arrived, broke down the door, but was unable to free him. The attendant called a policeman, who was also unable to help. Then a mechanic was fetched from a nearby garage to unscrew the seat.

As the professor was by this time exhausted and distraught, an ambulance was summoned. He was placed on a stretcher with the seat still stuck to him, but the ambulance men were unable to control their laughter and dropped him.

A second member was said to have been too upset by the death of a beloved pet to attend the gathering. He had left his cat in the care of an elderly aunt who had recently acquired a microwave oven. When the cat got soaked in a rainstorm, the old lady placed it in the microwave to dry out.

A third was in a state of shock after returning from a family holiday in Spain. On the way back, the grandmother died in the back of the car. Not wishing to leave her there with the children, he and his wife put her on the roof-rack covered in a car rug. At the border, the family got out for something to eat, and when they came back they found their car had been stolen.

Some 20 great stories would have been delivered on such curious topics as a piece of meat alleged to be 140 years old which still hangs on a Sheffield butcher's stall, a Dobermann Pinscher that choked on the bitten-off fingers of an intruder, and the sad story of paper-maker Reginald Pinfold who slipped into a giant pulveriser, never to be seen again. Members would have been asked to handle their newspapers gently.

However, although the meeting had failed to get started, the chairman did manage to get in a few words before he fell off the rostrum into the lap of a lady who had just bought an ice cream. He said we all love to hear stories that are outrageous, and he would very much like to hear from new members.

TASK

As you are keen to join the Tall Story Club you write to them for details of membership. Unfortunately, your letter fails to be delivered because the postman is run over by a lorry as he was walking around the outside of a ladder.

However, from a friend you learn that membership is entirely based on merit. To gain membership you are required to write two short dazzling tall stories of your own. When you have done this you have completed the task.

8 Making notes

Making notes is one of the most common and useful writing skills there is. It is basically the art of transforming a long and complicated message into a short and simple one. Although this sounds fairly easy, it does require practice to reach a good standard of skill. If we wish to take notes from a book or at a lecture, for example, we should be able to make a reasonably accurate summary of what we read or hear.

What use we make of notes depends on why we want to take them. If you are studying for an exam, or writing a project, or attending a class or a lecture, or just making plans for the future, you will find that being able to make accurate notes may well determine how well you succeed in your task. You cannot always depend on a teacher to write or to dictate notes for you.

Making notes from printed sources

Let us suppose we wish to make notes on the life of Bonnie and Clyde, the famous bank robbers. In a magazine we find a colourful account of their exploits. We read the first paragraph:

> Clyde, the he-man of the famous duo, was born Clyde Chestnut Barrow in March 1909. As was common in those far-off days, the Barrow parents produced eight children in total and Clyde was number six. Clyde's family was finger-licking poor and could hardly scrape a living from their Texas dirt farm. Try as they might, their crops refused to grow in the dry dust-soil. Eventually, they admitted defeat and sold out to an eager-faced property developer sporting a yellow suit, and moved to West Dallas in North East Texas.

If you read this through carefully, you will realise that it contains very little solid information. The first sentence gives us some facts about Clyde's birth, and the rest of the paragraph tells us about his family circumstances and their move to Dallas. Let us get out our knife and cut out the dead wood. What we are left with is this:

1. Clyde Chestnut Barrow, 1 of 8 children, born Mar 1909.
2. Parents poor Texan crop farmers. Sold farm to live in Dallas, Texas.

You can see that the facts have been taken out and the rest discarded. Notemakers are not interested in phrases such as 'finger-licking', or whether the soil was wet or dry, or to whom they sold their farm, or in the fact that the buyer was 'sporting a yellow suit'. We simply wish to record the main facts about Clyde's early childhood. On with the story:

> But let us not run too far ahead. We are back at the Barrow's farm and the young Clyde is blasting glass bottles to smithereens with his .22 hunting rifle. Soon the rifle lies broken on the ground—Clyde has missed the target and in vile uncontrollable temper has smashed his beloved rifle on a fence.
>
> Bart Dexter, friend of the Barrows and farm-neighbour, recalls Clyde as a boy. 'He used to come round to my place on a regular basis. He was a funny-looking kid, a bit soft looking. But he turned out as mean as a polecat. One day I caught him twisting the necks of my chickens. Another time he asks me would I like some firewood for free. The Lord preserve me if the son-of-a-bitch hadn't gone and chopped down my chicken house. I told him that one day he'd make a big reputation, and it wurnt be a reputation his Ma would be proud of.' Mr Dexter, with great personal regret, also recalls Clyde's obsession with other people's cars.

This might be an interesting account of the life of a delinquent, but for notemakers it can be reduced to a few words:

3. Delinquent child, quick-tempered, cruel to animals, passion for guns and cars.

To continue:

> As a child, Bonnie was in complete contrast. Born in October 1910 and christened Bonnie Parker, she was the daughter of a humble bricklayer. She grew up in a happy home and there was never an inkling that one day she would become a gun-toting cigar-smoking killer.
>
> She had outstanding physical beauty, with golden hair and bright cornflower-blue eyes. Her Aunt Agnes recalled: 'Bonnie was a lovely child. We used to picnic by the river and make daisy-chains together in the good weather. She was a child any parent would be proud of. No one could understand why she turned bad.'
>
> When she was 16 years old she fell in love and married a no-good childhood sweetheart named Roy Thornton. The marriage was a disaster and broke up within two years. Then Clyde came along, and in January 1930 the deadly pair set out on a crime trail that was to last over four years. Bonnie was just 19 years old.

From these three paragraphs we can get:

4. Bonnie Parker, daughter of bricklayer, born Oct 1910.
5. Happy childhood and unhappy 2-year marriage to Roy Thornton when 16.
6. Set up with Clyde in Jan 1930 when 19.

You can see that each note is numbered and set out neatly. You may also have noticed that some of the notes are not full sentences. Good notes are brief and exact.

We will recap and continue our story in note form:

<u>Bonnie and Clyde</u> <u>Date</u>

<u>Early years – Clyde</u>

1. Clyde Chestnut Barrow, 1 of 8 children, born Mar 1909.
2. Parents poor Texan crop farmers. Sold farm to live in Dallas, Texas.
3. Delinquent child, quick-tempered, cruel to animals, passion for guns and cars.

<u>Early years – Bonnie</u>

4. Bonnie Parker, daughter of bricklayer, born Oct 1910.
5. Happy childhood and unhappy 2-year marriage to Roy Thornton when 16.
6. Set up with Clyde in Jan 1930 when 19.

<u>Criminal activities</u>

7. 1932. Pair began career robbing small banks, cafés, filling stations.
8. Joined by Clyde's brother, Buck, and his wife Blanche. Other hoodlums join up.
9. 'The Barrow Gang' – driving stolen cars kill at least 13 people (mostly police officers) in several US states. Commit countless crimes.
10. July 1933. Ambushed by federal agents in wooded ravine. Blanche captured, Buck killed. <u>B</u> and <u>C</u> escape capture.
11. <u>C</u> known as 'The Texas Rattlesnake', <u>B</u> as 'Suicide Sal'.

Two more important points here. First, notice the main heading and date, and especially the smaller subheadings. These help to break up the notes into convenient sections. We have also introduced abbreviations in the form of *B* or *C* (for Bonnie and Clyde). This saves time and space.

Exercise Using a suitable subheading, complete the notemaking on the story of Bonnie and Clyde.

At 9 am on a beautiful summer's day in May 1934 in Gibsland, Louisiana, Bonnie and Clyde met their Maker. The proud possessors of a gleaming Ford V-8 sedan (stolen, of course), the tragic pair rounded a bend in a country road and met a vicious storm of bullets. Six lawmen, hiding in ambush and armed with machine-gun, rifles and shotgun, blasted the car. Over 200 rounds were fired and at least 50 rounds tore into the dancing bodies of Bonnie and Clyde.

When the Sheriff's men opened the car door they found them wrapped together in a grotesque embrace. Miraculously, Bonnie's golden hair was unmarked by the blood-bath. They had died the way they had wanted—together.

In the car they found this poem, written by Bonnie herself:

The Story of Suicide Sal

Some day they will go down together,
And they will bury them side by side.
To a few it means grief,
To the law it's relief,
But it's death to Bonnie and Clyde.

Taking notes at talks and lectures

Making notes from what is printed is much easier than taking notes from what is spoken. With the printed word you can read and reread until you are sure of the facts. In a lecture you only have one chance to get your notes on paper.

The best method to adopt is the same as we used for notemaking from printed sources, except you work that much quicker. The skill is to listen carefully to the speaker and then to jot down quickly the substance of what has just been said. There is no easy way of learning this technique—except by doing it.

We are now sitting in a lecture hall and the speaker is about to begin a talk on the future of the motor car. The following is an account of what the speaker said with your hand written notes. Before the speaker begins, you write down the heading:

The future of the motor car

Ladies and Gentlemen, I'm here today to discuss with you the future of the motor car. I realise that not everyone has a car but everyone is affected by the motor car in one way or another. But first it is necessary for me to outline briefly the car's history. (And looking at your cars in the car park on the way here. I got the impression that you know quite a bit about ancient cars!) To begin with,

History

we know that Sir Isaac Newton actually thought of it almost 250 years ago, although he only thought about it but never actually did anything of a

1. Newton first thought of car 250 years ago.

practical nature. (Some people have argued that Newton only thought about it after the apple had hit his head!) But if we think of the history of the car in petrol-propelled terms we must come forward to the end of the nineteenth century and say that without doubt the chief credit must go to Daimler, a German, who had built the first petrol-driven car by 1887.

2. Daimler built first petrol car – 1887.

In the same year, two young Frenchmen, Panhard and Levassor, introduced a clutch and gearbox mechanism which incredibly has hardly changed to the present day. Your car and mine has a gearbox that these two inventors would

3. Panhard and Levassor invented clutch and gears – 1887.

recognise instantly—that is a measure of their genius. In England, great strides had taken place in the introduction of the car but there was tremendous resistance from the horse transport operators who forced through a series of laws which deliberately slowed down the introduction of the car. These laws demanded that every moving car should be led by a man with a red flag and that its speed be restricted to four miles per hour. By the

4. In England, horse operators forced car drivers by law to:
   a) have a man in front with red flag
   b) drive at max 4 mph

way, driving here through the town centre, I suppose I averaged about eight miles per hour, so I suppose we have made some progress! However, Lanchester, a brilliant English inventor, introduced his first British car in 1895. This incorporated wire wheels and pneumatic tyres. This of course didn't

5. Lanchester intro first British car with wire wheels and inflated tyres – 1895.

make the car look much different but it did make it a lot more comfortable. Now let us come to the present day . . .

The present day

If we leave the lecture now, our notes would look like this:

> Date
>
> The future of the motor car
>
> History
>
> 1. Newton first thought of car 250 years ago.
> 2. Daimler built first petrol car – 1887.
> 3. Panhard and Levassor invented clutch and gears – 1887.
> 4. In England, horse operators forced car drivers by law to:
>   a) have a man in front with red flag
>   b) drive at max 4 mph
> 5. Lanchester intro first British car with wire wheels and inflated tyres – 1895.
>
> The present day

As you see, taking notes at a lecture is not easy. But it is possible if you stay calm and think clearly. The main point to keep in mind is that you are taking *notes* and not just copying every word the speaker says—even if this were possible.

Listen carefully until the speaker comes to the end of a particular section, and then write down in your own words a one-line summary of what was said. Leave out all the jokes, most of the examples, and the long descriptions, and concentrate on the *facts*.

Tips on note-making

1. The best type of notebook to buy is the A4 ring binder and separate note pad.
2. Do *not* put the writing paper directly into the ring binder. As each sheet of writing is completed on the pad, it is transferred to the binder.
3. *Do* write on both sides of the paper for economy.
4. Do *not* begin a new subject on the same sheet as another subject.
5. Be prepared to arrange your written sheets into subject order as you proceed. Divide your notebook into definite sections.
6. Neat layout is most important. Crowded, jumbled-up notes are not worth taking. Underline headings and key words.
7. Build up your notes in easy stages and number each point as you proceed. This makes the task easier and gives you confidence.
8. Use headings and subheadings for easy reference.
9. At the end of each set of notes make a record of the source of the information.
10. Always leave a few blank lines after each section to allow for any unexpected additional information.
11. Do *not* use abbreviations or single word reminders that you might later forget.
12. Remember that notemaking is to record the basic facts—so keep to the point, keep it short, and make sense.

Safety at work

TASK

Here is some practice at writing headings. In your notebook, write suitable headings for the sections numbered 4 to 11 (maximum six words). The first three have been done for you.

1 Cleanliness
Wash your hands frequently and especially before meals. If you have to work with oil, use a barrier cream to protect your hands.

2 Be tidy
Do not leave objects lying around where they are likely to cause accidents. Keep your workbench or desk clean and tidy—it makes for safer and more efficient working.

3 **Lifting heavy objects**
If an object is too heavy for you to move easily by yourself, don't be afraid to ask for help. If your job requires a lot of lifting, get proper instruction on how to do it properly. All too frequently, injuries are brought about by people attempting to move heavy objects without help and in the wrong way. Be sensible—and do it right.

If you work in an office, do not open more than one drawer of a filing cabinet at a time—otherwise the whole cabinet may topple on top of you!
If you have to move a typewriter, remember it is no light weight, so do not strain and do not rush. Be sure to have a space in which to put it down.

Do not let objects overhang the desk or table.

4 Wear the right clothes for the job.

Follow any rules about the wearing of protective clothing.

Certain operations require the use of eye-shields, visors, dust masks or ear defenders. Do not neglect to wear the appropriate protection. Better safe than sorry.

Do not wear tight skirts if you have to climb stairs or ladders, or badly worn or platform-soled shoes, which may cause you to trip.
Remember that long hair, neckties, belts, scarves, watches and rings can be caught up in moving machinery—sometimes with disastrous consequences for the wearer. Long hair should be tied well back and a careful check made of clothing to ensure that there are no loose ends.

5 Accidents can be caused by fooling about, so don't indulge in horse-play at your place of work.

Remember one slip could be enough to cause regret for the rest of your life.

Do not throw things or meddle with switches or levers; you may cause serious harm to yourself and to others. Remember that compressed air is a powerful working tool—not a toy; don't play around with it, it could be very dangerous.

6 If you use flammable materials, always handle them with extreme caution because of the fire risk. Do not smoke or use naked lights in any area where they are stored or used.

Many flammable materials, especially liquids, give off poisonous, flammable fumes which are explosive when mixed with air. They can also have a serious effect on your health if you breathe them. If in any doubt get advice from your supervisor.

7 Speed is commendable, but keep it under control. Do not run, you may trip and fall, injuring yourself; what is worse you may collide with someone else and cause an accident.

Use the designated gangways and pay strict attention to all *warning* signs—they are there for your protection.

8 In the course of your work you may have to handle toxic materials. Follow carefully any instructions for their handling and use. Where protective gloves, masks or eye-shields are required—*use them!* Do not take liberties with dangerous chemicals or materials.

9 Do not throw away lighted cigarette ends or matches, because these cause many serious fires. Think what you are doing and avoid the risk of fire—or worse!

10 Do not touch machinery unless you have been told to do so and have been instructed in its use. If there is a fault, report the matter to your supervisor and get proper advice and help. *Do not* attempt to fix it yourself.

Do not interfere with, or interrupt, other people who are using machinery; distraction can be dangerous.

Take particular care when near moving machinery and *do not* remove any protective guard or fencing, except under supervision.

11 Get to know where your nearest first-aid station is situated. If you injure yourself in any way, report it to the authorised person and obtain treatment. *Do not pass it off*, however trivial it may seem at the time—it could be important.

Health & Safety at Work Act 1974

TASK

An exam is looming and you anticipate at least one question on health and safety at work.

In your notebook prepare notes from this document:

Introduction

The purpose of the Health and Safety at Work etc Act is to provide the legislative framework to promote, stimulate and encourage high standards of health and safety at work.

The aim must be to promote safety awareness and effective safety organisation and performance. This can be achieved by schemes designed to suit the particular industry or organisation and by the accumulation of influences and pressures, operating at many levels, in a variety of ways, and from a number of directions.

Scope

All 'persons at work', whether employers, employees or self-employed, will be covered with the exception of domestic servants in a private household. About five million people such as those employed in education, medicine, the leisure industries and in some parts of the transport industry who have not been covered by previous health and safety legislation, will now be protected for the first time.

The legislation protects not only people at work, but also the health and safety of the general public who may be affected by work activities.

General duties

Duties of employers

Employers must safeguard, as far as is reasonably practicable, the health, safety and welfare of the people who work for them. This applies in particular to the provision and maintenance of safe plant and systems of work, and covers all machinery, equipment and appliances used.

Some examples of the matters which many employers will need to consider are:

- Is all plant up to the necessary standards with respect to safety and risk to health?
- When new plant is installed, is latest good practice taken into account?
- Are systems of work safe? Thorough checks of all operations, especially those operations carried out infrequently, will ensure that danger of injury or ill-health is minimised. This may require special safety systems, such as 'permits to work'.
- Is the work environment regularly monitored to ensure that, where known toxic contaminants are present, protection conforms to current hygiene standards?

Safety information and training

It is now the duty of employers to provide any necessary information and training in safe practices, including information on legal requirements. Employers will need to consider the specific training needs of their organisations with particular reference to processes with special hazards.

Duties to others

Employers must, so far as is reasonably practicable, have regard for the health and safety of self-employed or contractors' employees who may be working close to their own employees and also for the health and safety of the public who may be affected by their firm's activities. This covers, for example, the emission of noxious or offensive gases or dusts into the atmosphere or danger from machinery or plant where the public have access. Also included is the conveyance of dangerous substances and radiation entering public places. Employers must, so far as is reasonably practicable, conduct their activities so as to ensure that people other than their employees, for example, members of the public, are not exposed to risks to health and safety.

Duties of employees

Employees have a duty under the Act to take reasonable care to avoid injury to themselves or to others by their work activities, and to cooperate with employers and others in meeting statutory requirements. The Act also requires employees not to interfere with or misuse anything provided to protect their health, safety or welfare in compliance with the Act.

The likely effects of a nuclear attack

Light and heat

A nuclear explosion produces an intense flash of light lasting some seconds which would blind anyone seeing it. The heat flash can set fire to buildings up to some distance from the centre of the explosion depending upon the haziness of the atmosphere at the time. Skin exposed to the heat flash could suffer burns. But any shelter that withstands the blast would give protection against the heat flash. Any exposed parts of the shelter made of flammable materials could catch fire. Exposed plastic would not catch fire but might distort in the heat and this could weaken the resistance of the shelter to the subsequent blast wave.

Initial nuclear radiation (INR)

This very penetrating radiation is emitted from the fireball within one minute of the explosion. the distances from one megaton explosion and above, at which people require shielding from INR, are less than those distances at which there would be total destruction.

Blast

At the moment of explosion a blast wave would be generated, travelling at a tremendous speed and creating extremely strong winds which may last for several seconds. When the blast wave passes over a building the sudden increase of pressure and the following wind may cause the building either to explode or collapse.

Tremors

The tremors or shock waves from a ground blast extend for a short distance only and would not affect buildings beyond those already destroyed by the blast. The effect on shelters below the ground would depend on their ability to withstand ground movement and on the nature of the soil. Depth in the ground, shape and flexibility would be important.

Fallout

An explosion on or near the ground sucks up a large amount of earth and debris, which is vaporised as it rises to a great height and becomes highly redioactive. It then condenses to sand-like particles which are carried along by the wind and drop to the ground. The fallout can come down very near to the explosion or may be carried by the wind for hundreds of miles. The fallout dust is usually visible to the naked eye, but it emits ionising radiation rather like X-rays, which cannot be seen or felt. Radiation is dangerous and heavy doses cause sickness or death. Fallout dust remains radioactive for some days after the explosion–and can, in certain circumstances, still be dangerous after several weeks.

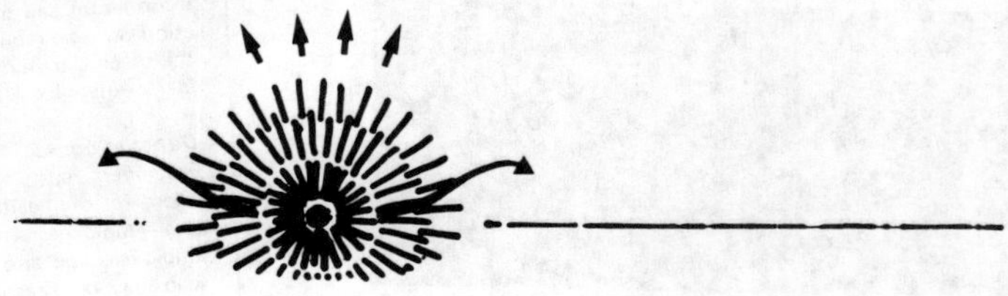

Bombs exploding on or near the ground

When a nuclear weapon explodes on or near the ground, a shock like a small earthquake goes through the ground. The earth vaporised into the fireball leaves a crater around the site of the explosion. The vaporised earth falls to the ground from half an hour to up to about a day later as radioactive fallout.

Bombs exploding in the air

When a nuclear bomb explodes in the air the blast effect is more marked: the area affected will be about 30 per cent greater than a ground-burst bomb of the same size. But with air-burst weapons there is no dangerous radioactive fallout–since the fireball does not touch the ground no earth is sucked up.

What happens to fallout after a nuclear attack

It is important to remember that the radiation emitted from fallout decreases as time passes, very rapidly at first and more slowly later. For example, after seven hours the radiation emitted will have fallen to one tenth of its strength and after two days to one hundredth. When the intensity has fallen sufficiently it will be safe to emerge from your shelter for short periods. You will be advised by radio when this is, and for how long you can stay outside. At first it might be safe to spend only an hour or so a day in the open but this safe period will gradually increase until it becomes safe to stay outside all the time. Even in the worst affected areas it might be safe to leave the shelter altogether after about two weeks and in most places this period would be very much shorter.

When outside the shelter no special clothing is required, but it would be advisable to wear outdoor clothing and wellington boots or stout shoes to avoid contamination of your indoor clothes. You should remove these clothes before re-entering the shelter.

The shelters described later on in this booklet offer differing degrees of protection against blast and against fallout. They will also provide protection against the heat flash provided no flammable materials are exposed.

No shelter is capable of protecting someone close to the site of a nuclear explosion, but for those who are far enough away to survive the initial effects, the principal danger after the explosion is from radioactive fallout.

Dense material around a shelter will lessen the risk of harm from radiation so long as you remain inside. Essentially, the thicker the material the better the protection. But some protective materials are more effective than others.

The protection given by buildings or shelters can be expressed as a **protective factor**. A typical house will reduce the power of the radiation to one fifteenth of that outside–this is called a protective factor of 15. Shelters constructed of the right materials can give a much greater protective factor than this.

The overall picture

If there were a nuclear attack, it is likely that some bombs might burst in the air, and some on or near the ground. Estimates suggest that around 5 per cent of the land area of the UK might suffer seriously from the effects of blast. We cannot, of course, know in advance where the bombs would fall, but about 80 per cent of the land area might suffer no blast effects at all. Any part of the country might suffer fallout and therefore radiation protection would be needed everywhere.

TASK

These extracts above and on page 98 are from a government booklet entitled 'Domestic Nuclear Shelters'. Take notes of the main ideas in the text and extract any useful information you can from the drawing.

Ugly face of football

Most of the fans who turned up for the sixth round cup tie at the City ground were good natured, but no football match can take place these days without the louts grabbing the headlines. While not wishing to make excuses for this mindless minority—and I stress both mindless and minority—I thought the officials at the City ground could have prevented some of the trouble had the sale of tickets been better organised.

One supporter—Graham White—returned home on Saturday evening without having seen the inside of the City ground. He broke his arm queuing for a ticket. He told me: 'I got to the ground really early, about 9 o'clock. Tickets were supposed to go on sale at half-ten. From what I've heard it was more like 12 o'clock before the first one was sold.'

While not wishing to make excuses for the mindless minority who go out of their way to spoil our national game, I think clubs could do a little more when it comes to organisation. One frustrated supporter told me after the game: 'I went to the North Side entrance, like it said in the press. Then after waiting an hour we were all told to go to the back of the queue on the South Side. That's where most of the United fans were queuing. There was bound to be trouble.'

And of course there was. Scuffles broke out, and people tried to force their way to the front of the queue. This is what happened to Graham White: 'I was right in front of the queue. They hadn't even started selling tickets and people were pushing forward. I lost my footing, got trampled on, and did my arm in.'

In fact, there was only one turnstyle open for the sale of tickets and, given the interest in the match and the expected crowd, this was painfully inadequate. As it turned out, the long wait in the queue proved too much for some fans. As soon as they got bored with their tribal chanting—*United–City–United–City–United–City*—skirmishes broke out. It seems that waiting your turn places too much stress on some football supporters these days!

The police arrived and 36 supporters were arrested, although some of the more experienced louts managed to avoid the long arm of the law.

A senior police officer put the whole sorry business into perspective: 'What we need to do is to keep the fans apart.

That's just for starters. The clubs should also ensure that there are enough stewards to supervise the crowd. It amazes me that clubs can spend a million pounds on one player and then penny pinch when it comes to staffing the grounds on match days.'

Meanwhile, Graham White nurses his broken arm and waits to see the highlights on TV. At least he's kept his sense of humour. 'Watching the game on telly should be safer. Unless I break my leg in the stampede to get to the best armchair.'

TASK

You are writing a project on football hooliganism and you come across this newspaper article. Make notes of any useful information contained in the article or any conclusions you can draw from what the people told the reporter. If there are any points you can add from your own knowledge or experience, then include these too.

Smoking statistics

Cigarette smoking habits in Great Britain: by age and sex, 1972 and 1980

Percentages

	Age												All aged 16 and over	
	16–19		20–24		25–34		35–49		50–59		60 +			
	1972	1980	1972	1980	1972	1980	1972	1980	1972	1980	1972	1980	1972	1980
Men														
Current non-smokers														
• Never or only occasionally smoked	53	62	36	48	27	34	22	27	16	18	18	19	25	30
• Ex-regular smokers	4	5	9	8	17	18	24	27	30	35	35	45	23	28
Current smokers	43	32	55	44	56	47	55	45	54	47	47	36	52	42
Women														
Current non-smokers														
• Never or only occasionally smoked	57	63	44	51	41	43	41	44	41	39	66	57	49	49
• Ex-regular smokers	4	4	8	9	10	13	11	13	12	17	9	19	10	14
Current smokers	39	32	48	40	49	44	48	43	47	44	25	24	41	37

TASK

A great deal of information can be extracted from statistics. Looking very carefully at the table above, make notes under the following headings:

1. General smoking trends in the 1970s.
2. The smoking habits of the young and old in 1980.
3. Smoking trends of men and women aged 16 to 19 between 1972 and 1980.

Pets

TASK

Make brief notes on the information below.

102

Pets and their needs

The first necessity for any animal is a healthy start in life. Proper care and handling during the first few vulnerable weeks of an animal's life are vital. Always buy puppies from reputable breeders or the owner of the bitch. Unscrupulous puppy 'dealers', street pet markets and substandard pet shops inflict untold harm on the animals they handle and create misery for the new owners whose pets hardly ever thrive.

Their needs later on are simple. Regular food and water of course, but feeding need not be such a major expense as some people imagine. Dogs don't generally need the very high protein 'luxury' diet that many of them become used to. A balanced mixture of protein in the form of tinned meat or fresh cheap cuts, and carbohydrate in the form of biscuit, meal or bread is perfectly adequate. An occasional raw marrow bone is usually welcomed. Cats require a high protein diet, but there is no necessity to buy the highest quality meat or fish – fussy cats have usually had their tastes created by their owners.

Exercise is another must. Dogs need exercise in the fresh air every day if they are to remain healthy and lively. Basic training in good behaviour, to walk properly on a lead and to come when called, make for happier relations with your dog too. Cats and smaller animals must have access to the outdoors.

Grooming and cleaning is a process which all animals enjoy and long-haired animals need. It is occasionally necessary to deal with fleas. There are several effective products on the market and the treatment is as straightforward as it is essential.

Human company is vital to the wellbeing of pets – dogs in particular. Don't subject your dog to long periods of isolation.

Pets and the law

You may very well be affected by one of the many laws relating to animals whether or not you are a pet owner. Did you know, for instance, that if you hit a dog with your car, you must report it to the police? If you own a pet, then it's even more important that you are familiar with the rules.

When you first acquire a dog, you must provide it with a collar and clear identification and buy a dog licence from a post office. Do not allow your dog to stray; if you do and it causes a traffic accident, then you may be faced with a huge bill for damages. Similarly, if you own a vicious or dangerous animal, it is your responsibility to see that the public is protected by keeping it under proper control. Some local authorities impose restrictions on where animals are allowed to be taken, and it is almost always the case that dogs in public places must be kept on a lead.

The fouling of footpaths by dogs is not allowed in many urban areas, and local authorities are becoming more strict about imposing fines on the owners of transgressing dogs. In rural areas, farm livestock must be protected by the law, and if your pet dog chases or molests farm animals, you could face heavy fines. Your dog also faces the danger of being shot by the farmer, who would be perfectly within his rights to do so.

A final reminder – cruelty to animals is illegal and cruelty isn't exclusively the more violent acts of animal abuse. Neglect, abandonment or lack of care resulting in actual suffering can be equally as cruel and just as severely punished.

Many of the laws relating to animals have been designed for their protection. By strict observation of the laws, you would be helping the country's domestic pets lead happier and more secure lives.

9 Letters and messages

Although the telephone is being used more and more, the occasional letter we write is still important. In fact, there are occasions when letters are a superior form of communication. If we want to tell someone how sorry we are about a loss they have suffered, a short, kind letter might be an easier way of doing it than a message over the phone.

There are letters that can change our lifestyle completely. Letters from a relation living abroad might lead us to emigrate (or not to). Letters to penfriends and holiday friends have led to friendships and marriage! Letters to employers may determine whether we are invited to a job interview and sometimes guarantee that we will definitely *not* be invited. Whichever way we look at it, letter-writing skills are worth cultivating.

Business letters

When we write a letter to a company we are writing what is called a business letter. If the company writes to us or to another company they too are writing a business letter. Letters that we exchange with our friends and relatives are called personal or private letters.

For most of us, the need to write business letters is happily not too frequent, but when the time does arrive we ought to be in a position to produce a letter that will succeed in its purpose. This means writing a letter that will get us what we want, whether this takes the form of a request for, say, leaflets or information, or for something more important like a job interview. Whatever the purpose of our business letter, getting our ideas down first on paper and then sorting them out in logical order before presenting them in a readable way, is as important in business letter writing as in most other kinds of writing.

Writing a letter to a firm or to an organisation does not require a special language, but it does require you to write clearly and accurately. There are, however, certain rules to be learnt, rules that once learnt will enable you to write a business letter fairly easily.

The most important feature of a business letter is the way it is laid out. On page 104 is a diagram of a typical letter written by an individual to a company. It should be noted that although this is one of the accepted layouts, there are other layouts that can be used equally well.

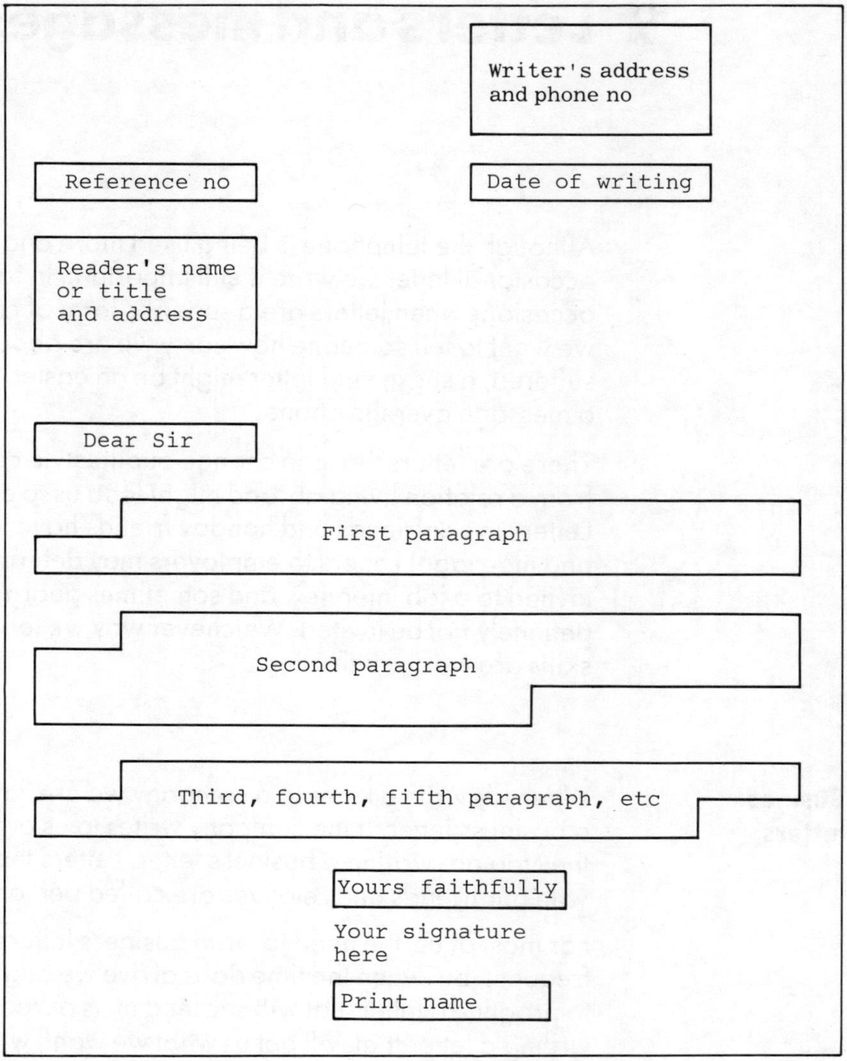

There are some important points to be made here:

- Write all addresses clearly, and check later for accuracy.
- Always include your reference number if the company has given you one in previous correspondence.
- If you start the letter 'Dear Sir' or 'Dear Madam' then end the letter 'Yours faithfully'.
- If you start the letter 'Dear Mrs Smith' or 'Dear Jane' then end the letter 'Yours sincerely' (use Ms instead of Mrs if you don't know whether the reader is married or single).

- The first paragraph should come straight to the point and tell the reader the purpose of the letter. For example:

  Thank you for writing to me and explaining why you refuse to insure my motor bike. I am sure that you are wrong about this for the following reasons.

- The remaining paragraphs should deal with the different points in logical order.
- The last paragraph should briefly sum up the final position:

  I hope you will reconsider renewing my insurance, and I look forward to a favourable reply.

- Print your name in neat letters under your signature.

Let us work through a series of letters between a Miss Lewis and 'Simpsons', a mail order company. Miss Lewis sends for a wrist watch and gets this reply:

Simpsons Mail Order Company

25/30 Great George Street
Manchester M16 5AN
Telephone 061 584 3924

13 December 19--

Your ref: DLP/FND

J F Lewis
18 Malborough Avenue
Harbiton
LONDON
L27 2EJ

Dear Sir or Madam

ORDER NO 78D 869

Thank you for your order for a Marco Digital Quartz Watch and your remittance of £14.95, including postage and packing.

I have instructed our Despatch Department to forward you the article without delay.

Yours faithfully

J Sands

Jeremy Sands
Director

Four weeks later Miss Lewis has not received her watch. She replies:

18 Malborough Avenue
Harbiton
LONDON
L27 2EJ

Ref : DLP/FND

13 January 19--

Jeremy Sands, Director
Simpsons Mail Order Company
25/30 Great George Street
MANCHESTER
M16 5AN

Dear Mr Sands

On the 13 December 19-- you wrote to tell me that you had told your Despatch Department to send me my wrist watch. I have <u>not</u> received this article.

The watch is a Marco Digital Quartz, and the order number is 78D 869. I sent a Postal Order for £14.95 and I have the counterfoil in my possession.

I do hope you will look into this matter urgently.

Yours sincerely

J. Lewis

Miss Jane Lewis

Three weeks later Jane gets this reply (to save space the addresses have been deleted):

> Dear Miss Lewis
>
> ORDER NUMBER 78D 869
>
> Thank you for your letter informing us that you have not received your Marco Digital Quartz Watch.
>
> I have made the fullest enquiries on your behalf and I have discovered that the watch in question is no longer in stock. I therefore suggest that we forward you a more expensive model in our Marco range.
>
> In view of this, I am asking you to send me an extra £5.50 for our Marco Digital Quartz and Calculator Watch (Order Number 78D 870). When we receive the money we will send you the article immediately.
>
> Yours sincerely
>
> J Sands
>
> Jeremy Sands
> Director

Exercise

If you were Jane, what would you do now?

Jane decides to send a 'stronger' letter to Simpsons because she thinks (quite rightly) she is being treated unfairly. Write a business letter on Jane's behalf to persuade Simpsons to either send the original watch or to return the money. Leave a space for Jane to sign the letter.

Writing for a job

If you write a letter as part of a job application you have to be sure that the letter is going to be received favourably. An attractive letter may not guarantee a job, but it just might get you to an interview.

The first ingredient of an attractive letter is its relevance to the job. You must give an employer a good reason to invite you for an interview, so it is important to read the job advertisement carefully and to write your letter in a way that is appealing to that particular employer.

The second ingredient is to include any unusual quality you have or any achievement you have attained. At school, did you captain any team or belong to any interesting club or society? Have you gained any award, however unusual, in anything? Have you ever held a responsible position or done any work for charity? What work have you done full-time or part-time? As a school leaver, an employer might be more impressed if you have worked successfully at a part-time job or at a creative hobby, rather than if you have a Grade 3 or a Grade 4 in a CSE subject.

As for the letter itself, the usual rules of good letter writing still apply. Here is an example of how a young person might write for a job in a large hotel restaurant:

17 Seafield Avenue
Mannofield
ABERDEEN
AB6 5MP

Telephone 858 2362

12 September 19--

Reference: ST/TW

Mr G McCleish
Personnel Officer
'Ambleside' Hotel
Ambleside Road
ABERDEEN AB8 3FJ

Dear Mr McCleish

I am very interested in applying for the job of Junior Chef which you advertised in the Aberdeen Evening News on 10 September 19--.

I am $16\frac{1}{2}$ years old and I left school at the end of the Summer term. I passed CSE examinations in three subjects which are English and Mathematics (Grade 3) and Home Economics (Grade 1). I am also keen on sport and I was captain of the school Swimming team in my final year. I liked the responsibility of being captain.

It has been my lifelong ambition to work in catering and I know that you have an excellent reputation in the town. I would be pleased if you would give me an opportunity to show you how keen I am to learn the trade.

In my spare time I have been helping out in a small café for the last eight months and I have gained some useful work experience. I also take an interest in home cooking and I have been learning about the confectionery trade from my uncle who is a qualified chef.

I shall be pleased to provide any further information you require and I am available to come for an interview at any time.

Yours sincerely

Alex Henderson

Mr Alex Henderson

You will notice that the letter is fairly short and to the point. It contains all the important details and it might give Alex a slight advantage over a better qualified applicant whose letter is too long or carelessly written.

The curriculum vitae

(pronounced cur-ric-u-lum-veet-i)

It might be a good idea to prepare yourself what is called a curriculum vitae (often referred to as the CV). This is simply an outline history of your life which would be of interest to employers. There are two occasions when you would include a CV with your letter of application:

1. If you are writing to a firm 'on spec', hoping to get a job through your own initiative.
2. If the employer does not provide an official application form.

It has a third useful purpose. If an employer asks you to complete an application form on the day of the interview, it can be embarrassing if you can't remember all those details—exam grades, dates, etc. A resourceful candidate would always carry a spare CV.

This is what might be included in a Curriculum Vitae for a young person:

Curriculum Vitae

Name
Address (including phone no)
Secondary schools attended (name of school, town, dates)
Colleges attended (name of college, town, dates)
Qualifications (name of exam, subject and grade)
Other qualifications, attainments or awards
Jobs held, including part-time and short training schemes (dates and titles)
Interests and hobbies
Referees: names, addresses and phone numbers of three people who would write useful references for you (ask them first)

You will notice that for a school leaver the educational details immediately follow the address. If you are an older person you would place your most recent qualifications and industrial experiences much higher in the list to give them prominence.

Exercise

Prepare yourself a Curriculum Vitae. When you are satisfied that it is perfect, get it typed and keep it safe.

Personal letters

A personal letter is laid out in a similar way to a business letter, except that references and the reader's name and address are removed. We are free to write almost anything we wish and in any style we choose. However, we are still communicating and therefore we have to try to write clearly.

Here is a short letter written by a young North Sea diver to his 12 year old sister:

UK North Sea Area
Magnus Field
North Sea Sector

18 February 19--

Dear Sis

Did you get my postcard I sent from shore? I'm surprised you haven't written back. I'll tell Mom if you don't write me soon. We should be staying on this rig for a few months so you haven't got any excuses now, have you!

It's unbelievably cold here because we're hundreds of miles north of Scotland, and the sea is rough all the time. (I bet you don't know why the North Sea is so rough – I'll tell you in my next letter). But the rig itself is very safe. It's like a small village with shops and cafés.

We dive in about 150 metres of sea water one day in every three. We wear water-heated suits and this keeps us very warm and cosy. You'd be amazed how dark it is down there – you can't see your hand in front of your face! Definitely not the place for cheeky sisters who don't write to their brothers!

Guess what? I bought a little present for you in one of the shops on the rig. It's something you've always wanted, but I'm not going to send it unless you write to me NOW!!!

Your brother

Toby

PS You can tell Paul I've got him some rock specimens for his collection.

Notes and messages

These should be kept short and accurate.

Here is a note someone has left for the milkman. What is wrong with it?

> Please deliver 2 pints of sterilised and ordinary tomorrow.
> Also 3 small bags of red and white potatoes. Thanks.

Should the milkman deliver two pints of sterilised and two pints of ordinary, or one of each? Does the customer want six small bags of potatoes or three? What does tomorrow actually mean? If the note was written early that morning, then it does mean tomorrow. If it was written the evening before, it means today. What a mess! Let us rewrite the note:

> Please deliver on Thursday:
>
> 2 pints ordinary
> 2 pints sterilised
> 2 small bags white potatoes
> 1 small bag red potatoes
>
> Thanks.

Although these short notes take only seconds to write, it is even more necessary to write clearly and accurately. Mistakes are easy to make and difficult to put right. This is a telegram from a pregnant wife to her husband who is working abroad:

```
COME HOME IMMEDIATELY NEW CAR ARRIVING FRIDAY BABY
EXPECTED SOON JOHNSONS ARE DELIVERING
```

Exercise

1 Rewrite the telegram to make sense.
2 You are going on a week's holiday. Write a note for the newsagent cancelling your newspapers.

The memo

When a message is written by an employee to another employee it is called a **memo** (short for memorandum). Memos are just notes written in a particular way. They are set out under these headings:

MEMO

From ....

To ....

Date ....

Subject ....

You are employed as a shop assistant in a large store. A customer walks out of the shop without paying for a pocket calculator and the manager asks you to explain what happened in a memo. This is how you might set it out:

MEMO

FROM Alex Johnson, shop assistant

TO Mr Roberts, manager

DATE 18 June 19--

SUBJECT Theft of pocket calculator

1. At 3 pm on Wednesday 17 June a man asked me to show him the model 202 Superknow pocket calculator, price £12.95.
2. He looked at it and then asked to see model 204 in the same range.
3. When I returned with the second calculator the man had left the shop with the 202 model.
4. I told my supervisor, Mrs Price, who phoned the police.
5. The police came and I gave a statement at 3.45 pm.

Exercise

You are an important member of the Government.

The Employment Secretary asks you to send him a five-point memo suggesting ways to increase job opportunities for young people.

Tips on letter writing

1. The key to good letter writing is politeness. Try to keep on friendly terms with your reader.
2. If you are asked any questions or requests by letter, always check that you have dealt with them *before* you seal the reply envelope.
3. Check that all addresses are complete and accurate. If your handwriting is poor, print the addresses in *block capitals.*
4. If you are sending other documents with your letter, then say so under your signature. (Enclosed: Curriculum Vitae and stamped addressed envelope.)
5. If you write a letter of complaint, do not be rude or abusive. Remain sensible but firm. *Do not* send any documents that prove your arguments (just say that you have them).
6. *Do not* send important documents through the post if you can avoid it (school reports, birth certificate, exam certificates). Keep the original and send a photocopy.
7. Unless it is urgent, save money and send letters second class.
8. If you want the envelope to be marked 'Confidential' or 'Personal', this should be written in the top left-hand corner.
9. If you want to be extra sure that your letter will be delivered, send it by *Recorded Delivery Service.*
10. If you must send money or valuables through the post, send them by *Registered Letter Service.*
11. If you return goods to a company by letter or parcel, ask for a *receipt of posting* at the Post Office. This service is free.

Packing

TASK

You are invited to a friend's house for a three-day visit. Make a note of the items you should carry with you, and what you should pack in a small suitcase.

Lynden

TASK

You are driving through Lynden and your car breaks down in Wentworth Park Avenue. Investigating, you discover oil seeping from the engine, along with clouds of billowing steam. You push the car into a parking space in Wood Road and find the nearest garage, which is closed. You decide to write a note and slip it through their letter box. The garage is situated at the junction of Heath Road and Church Hill Road.

Explain what has happened and request a tow to the garage for repair. Draw a rough sketch from your street map to help them locate your car (a red Mini—LDT 364R).

Confessions of an unlucky man

116

It never rains but it pours. The truth of this saying came home to me last week. On Monday morning I crashed my car into a lamp post after skidding on ice. The car was a write-off. Later, the hospital doctors told me that I had broken my right leg in two places. When the police told me I was to be prosecuted for drunken driving the next day I couldn't believe my ears. The last drink I had was at a party the evening before. Mind you, I did have a lot to drink and I behaved so badly that my wife ran off with another man, and I haven't seen her since. Then on Thursday I was told that my house had been broken into, ransacked and vandalised, and that my wife had later sold off all the furniture in an auction. Then came the last straw. On Saturday, my brother sent me a telegram from Canada saying he was arriving in two days' time for a short visit. He was looking forward to staying with us.

TASK

Send him an international telegram at once to cancel the visit. Explain as much as you can in 30 words. Begin the message with his name and address which is:

MICHAEL WILLIAMS 4097 CASTLE STREET ONTARIO CANADA

British TELECOM **Telegram**

POST OFFICE INTERNATIONAL TELEGRAM

BLOCK LETTERS THROUGHOUT PLEASE NO PUNCTUATION

TO ____________________

Memo

MEMO

FROM The Managing Director

TO All employees

DATE 31 January

SUBJECT Fire precautions

In order to reduce the possibility of death or serious injury through fire, the management has decided, after due consultation, to recommend that all employees, on hearing the fire bell ring, should stop work immediately and leave the room in order to effect an escape. The management recommends that in the event of any employee discovering the ordinary stairways blocked or smoke-filled that he, the employee, should use the fire escape forthwith and under no circumstances consider using the lifts.

TASK

This memo was sent to the employees of a large department store. Unfortunately, half the staff found it difficult to understand. Rewrite the memo so that the staff would know exactly what to do in case of fire.

Good fortune?

Nineteen year old unemployed Cyril Bradley has a problem. He and his best friend, merchant seaman Trevor Shaw, have picked all eight draws on a football coupon and stand to win a fortune.

The problem is that Cyril forgot to post the coupon! Let Cyril explain:

'I'm real sick in my stomach. Trevor and me, we picked out all eight draws. I phoned him yesterday at Portsmouth to tell him we've hit the jackpot, and he went and bought himself a couple of £100 suits. He was saving this money for his girl's engagement ring.

'Then I found the envelope and coupon in my pocket—I must have posted a blank envelope. I'm real sick.'

Cyril has the job of writing to his mate who is now at sea. And to rub salt into the wound, his ship is called *Good Fortune*.

TASK

Imagine you are Cyril. Using your own address, write a letter to Trevor to tell him the latest news.

Applying for a job

TASK

You see an advertisement for a job you have always wanted. Using your own name and address, write a letter of application. The employer is a Mr T Edwards, 239 New Valley Road, CRESSLINGTON, C30 6TC.

Mailbox

Our 'Grouse Corner' this week turns its attention to the young generation. Readers have sent in their 'grouses', and we publish a sample.

The good old days

Dear Grouse Corner,

If young people spent as much time helping old people as they do listening to pop music and having a good time, the world would be a better place to live in.

When I was young I was expected to stay at home and help with the housework. These days I see gangs of young people roaming around the town centre with nothing to do except look like zombies with wires sticking out of their ears. They even have to listen to pop music when they walk down the street!

Let's get back to the good old days, I say, when young people were called children and not 'teenagers'.

Mrs Rathbone

Eye for an eye

Let's stop pussyfooting around and examine the facts as they are and not as we want them to be.

Street crime is increasing in leaps and bounds, so are burglary, vandalism, divorce, child abuse, alcoholism, drug addiction, rape and glue sniffing. You name it, and it's on the increase.

And what do these crimes have in common? They are crimes mainly committed by young people.

Rupert Shaw

The world owes them a living

Again in the paper tonight there is a picture and story of a group of miserable-looking teenagers bemoaning the fact they haven't got anything to do in the evenings, so they expect the ratepayers to cough up thousands of pounds for a youth club to be built for them. Poor little souls!

All we had in our day was the street or a friend's front room with a record player on which we played our precious records—precious because it took us weeks to save for just one 78 record. But we had a good time and we behaved.

I never had a record player. Only well-off people could afford them. We didn't crave one, and that was that. At least we were free of debt and when you are free of that you're happy.

We were just like all young people. We thought we knew it all. But we never expected the world to owe us a living. In the War we got on with our lives, hoping to turn the world into a better place. What has gone wrong? Why does this generation think that the world owes them a living?

Miss J. Worrall

Labour camps
We hear a lot these days about teenage unemployment. I know there are lots of nice young people who would really like a job, but I'm sure there are thousands of teenagers who prefer to scrounge off the State.

In my day unemployment was almost as bad as it is now, but it was actually much worse in the way it affected the individual. Nobody starves these days or goes about in bare feet. I remember eating bread and dripping for my breakfast and we used to burn old tin cans in the grate to keep us warm in those terrible winters.*

I'd like to see labour camps set up in the countryside. We could send all the young unemployed to work on the land and help this country to grow its own food.

The Devil makes work for idle hands to do. This is my favourite saying.

Bert Wood

* *Editor's note:* Burning tin cans in coal fires was practised by many poor families. It was thought the metal reflected the heat into the room.

R U 18?
This teenage drinking is an abomination. I called in my local on Saturday night and I saw hordes of teenage under-age drinkers guzzling beer and spirits like old soldiers. There were a couple of youngsters I swear could not have been more than 14.

What I can't understand is, where do these young alcoholics get their money from? I don't suppose any of them have tried to get work while the pubs are open!

Concerned

Robbed and beaten
Last Saturday night I was robbed and beaten by a gang of young hairless hooligans on the top deck of a No 16 bus. I have a broken nose, two broken front teeth, a cracked rib and numerous bruises. I was also robbed of my redundancy money of £195.

If any of these hooligans are reading this letter (if they can read) I hope they feel ashamed and guilty, although I have a feeling they couldn't care less.

I am 45 years old, unemployed and married with two young children.

Les Phillips

TASK

As a young person you feel that you must put your point of view forward to deal with at least some of these criticisms.

Write a letter for publication of at least five paragraphs to: The Editor, 'Mailbox', Evening News, Newspaper House, City Centre Boulevard, CC1 6AB. Use your own name and address.

Note: Jot down as many points as you can and get them into some sort of order *before* you start your letter.

We want to work!

We want to work!

Are you one of the many unemployed? Are you doing all you can to find a job?

You will be pleased to hear that your local paper will be publishing a special feature called 'We want to work'.

For the cost of a packet of cigarettes – £1 – you can tell a prospective employer about yourself. You are allowed a maximum of 16 words. Box numbers are not permitted and you must include your name and address or telephone number within the advertisement (maximum of 7 letters per box).

Now complete the details below: One word per box.

				COST ONLY
				£1
				FOR 16 WORDS

TASK

Complete the form as instructed. Practice on a separate sheet of paper and count your words before you commit them on the form.

10 Filling in forms

Believe it or not, forms were invented to make life easy for us. Yet many of us find the prospect of filling in forms either worrying or boring. This is unfortunate because forms that are carelessly or incorrectly completed can put us to a lot of inconvenience and delay and might get us into serious trouble. Giving false information on a driving licence application, for example, can cost £1000 or two years imprisonment!

If we think about it, the more important forms require a signature, and we all know that we should *not* sign anything unless we are certain that what we do sign is true. We must also be aware of the consequences of our form filling, especially forms involving loans such as hire purchase and credit agreements.

A second reason why we should take extra care with forms is because they are nearly always kept in filing cabinets or the information they contain is held in computers. Unlike most things we write which eventually get lost (letters, postcards, notes, etc), forms always remain as a permanent record of what we wrote on a particular day; so we must try to be accurate and neat and not write anything we will later regret.

Completing the form

If we have a blank form in front of us, we must first look it over to see which sections we should complete. We should then read through any notes that are printed for our guidance.

Some forms contain sections that are not meant to be completed. These are usually headed 'Official Use Only' and we must be careful to leave these blank.

On page 122 is part of a form for an application for a visitor's passport. If you look at the top right-hand corner you will see the heading 'For Official Use Only', and we must not write anything within the black boxes. The remainder of the form contains other pitfalls:

- We should use a ball point pen
- We must use BLOCK CAPITALS where instructed
- We must read the notes *before* we answer some of the questions

Form VP **APPLICATION FOR BRITISH VISITOR'S PASSPORT (FOR PERSON WHO MUST BE AGED 8 OR OVER)**

FILE NUMBER

VALID FOR CERTAIN COUNTRIES ONLY (see Section 8)
FEE £5.50 DOCUMENTS REQUIRED (see Note (viii))
TO BE COMPLETED IN INK (PREFERABLY BY BALL POINT PEN) BY THE APPLICANT (FOR A CHILD UNDER SIXTEEN THIS SHOULD BE A PARENT) AFTER FIRST CAREFULLY READING THE NOTES ON PAGES 3 AND 4

FOR OFFICIAL USE ONLY
Passport number
Date of issue

1 PERSON FOR WHOM PASSPORT IS REQUIRED

SURNAME (IN BLOCK CAPITALS) State whether Mr., Mrs., Miss or Ms.

Height .....ft ......ins

Private address in the United Kingdom, Isle of Man or Channel Islands. (IN BLOCK CAPITALS)

Christian Names (or Forenames) in full (IN BLOCK CAPITALS)

Height (See Note (vi)) ....metres

Postcode

Date of Birth | Age

Maiden Surname (IN BLOCK CAPITALS) if applicant is a woman who is or has been married

Town of Birth | Country of Birth

Visible distinguishing marks

2 PARTICULARS OF WIFE/HUSBAND (if to be included in the same Visitor's Passport)(See Note (v)(a))

Christian Names (or Forenames) and Surname in full (IN BLOCK CAPITALS) | Date of Birth

Height .....ft ......ins

Town of Birth | Country of Birth

Height (See Note (vi)) ....mete

Maiden Surname (IN BLOCK CAPITALS)

Visible distinguishing marks

3 PARTICULARS OF CHILDREN, UNDER 16, IF TO BE INCLUDED IN PASSPORT
(including adopted or step children) NOTE:- Section 4 must also be completed and signed

Forenames (in full)	Surname	Date of Birth	Sex	Relationship to Applicant

4 PARENT'S CONSENT FOR PERSON UNDER 18 (see Note (v)(e) on Page 3)

I(full names)...of (address)..of
....being the (relationship)..................hereby request that he/she/they* be granted the facilities
(name(s))..
here applied for. I declare that my rights in respect of the child/children* have not been limited in any way by the order of any court having jurisdiction over him/her/them*

*Delete as appropriate Signature...

- We must ask ourselves what 'visible distinguishing marks' actually means
- We must get the permission and signature of one of our parents if we are under 18
- We must be sure that the 'deletions' have been done

Considering all the mistakes we could make, we would be wise to make a few notes on a separate sheet of paper *before* we transfer them to the form.

Exercise Get hold of a few forms from a Post Office and practice form filling for yourself.

Job application forms

Without doubt, these are the most important forms we are ever likely to meet. How we fill in the form may determine whether we are invited to an interview, so we must be sure to do a first-class job. A neat and accurate form will not guarantee an interview, but a scruffy and inaccurate one will certainly be rejected.

When you receive the application form proceed in this way:

1. Read the form carefully and follow any instructions given to you.
2. Think carefully about your answers before you write them on a separate sheet of paper.
3. Give yourself time to think over what you have written. If you think of a way of improving your answers, now is the time to do it.
4. Check everything for spelling, punctuation and grammar. Show your work to someone to check for errors.
5. Copy your answers neatly and carefully onto the application form. Follow instructions exactly (using block capitals, black ink, etc).
6. Check that you have answered *all* the appropriate questions.
7. If possible, take a photocopy. This will be important as a preparation for the interview. It will also be helpful for future use.

When the form is finished, it should look neat and accurate. This cannot be emphasised too much. It may be your first contact with the employer, and first impressions are important.

Report forms

In factories and offices, forms are used for all kinds of purposes. A 'work progress' form, for example, is used to record the progress of a particular job as it passes from one department to another until the job is completed. The purpose of the form is to tell anybody at any time exactly what has been done by whom.

Another important document is an accident report form. These forms are completed after an accident has caused injury. An example appears on page 124.

Compiling an accident report form

If we are asked to complete an accident report form we must try to record the facts accurately. First, on a separate sheet of paper, make a list of the events as they occurred in the correct order; then write a rough description of the events and action taken; check for accuracy and ask someone to read it through; and finally write it neatly onto the form using drawings as an aid to understanding.

Accident report form

Name of injured person: PERCY SPOONER

Place and time of accident: D shop 3pm Date: 15 March 19--

Description of accident:

Percy Spooner was pushing a trolley of metal ingots along gangway 8 when he slipped and banged his head against the side of No 2 machine (see drawing).

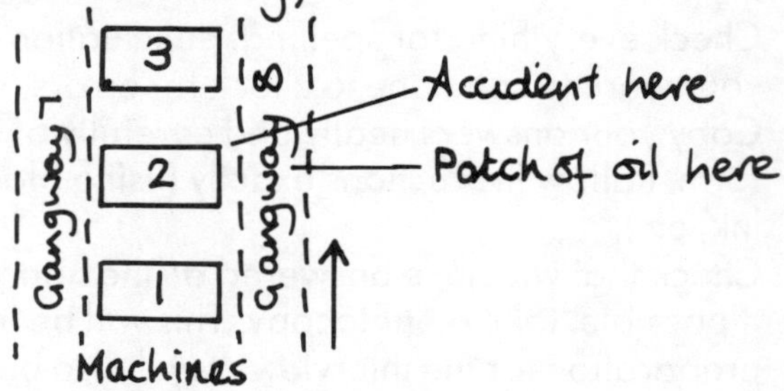

On further examination, a patch of machine oil was found on the floor (about the size of a football) which probably caused Mr Spooner to slip.
He received a 2-inch long cut to his forehead about an inch above his left eye. The wound bled freely.

Action taken:

No 2 machine was stopped immediately and disconnected from the electricity supply. I attempted to stop the bleeding by pressing the edges of the wound together. When the bleeding stopped I applied a first-aid dressing and sticking plaster. I took him to the First-Aid station on the ground floor where the wound was cleaned and dressed. Mr Spooner returned to D Shop at 3.55pm.

Completed by: RALPH TURNER Department: Production

Signature: R-Turner Date: 16 March 19--

Tips for form fillers

1. If possible, always ask for *two* forms. A spare is always useful.
2. If possible, insist on taking the form away with you to complete in your own time. Don't be panicked into form filling.
3. Do *not* rush into filling a form. Read and understand it first.
4. If the form is important, *do* write the information on a separate sheet of paper first. Then copy it onto the form.
5. *Do* complete the form lightly in pencil. When satisfied, fill in with ink. When the ink is dry, rub out any pencil marks.
6. If you are asked to answer a question, answer it. Do *not* leave questions unanswered. If the question does not apply to you, write 'Not applicable' or 'None'.
7. If a signature is required, check that you have signed the form. If the form is unsigned it will be sent back to you.
8. A signature is your own special mark. Do *not* write Mr or Miss in front of it or print it out in capitals.
9. Always give a completed form a last look over *before* you send it off.
10. Try to get a photocopy of your really important forms. You can find a photocopying service shop in most town centres.

Application form

TASK

Look at the completed job application form. How many mistakes can you spot? Make a list of them in your notebook. (The form is on page 126.)

Are there any other items you think an employer might object to?

APPLICATION FORM (Please use block letters throughout)

Application for the post of APRENTICE ELECTRICIAN

Surname JONES Other names MICHAEL NEIL

Current address 125 Antrobus Road Strangeways Manchester

Date of birth 31 January 1966 Marital status NO

Nationality English Sex Mail

Previous employment

Firm	From	To	Job title
Renshaw Electronics PLC	2/9/82	30/2/83	MSC Training in Electronics

Education

School	From	To	Qualifications
Grove Primery	2/9/71	7/7/77	CSEs English (Grade 2)
Whitworth Comprehensive	3/9/78	3/7/82	Maths (Grade 4) Geography (Grade 2)

Do you hold a driving licence? No Have you the use of a car? No

Have you been employed with us previously?

Have you suffered any serious illness or physical disability of which your employer should know (eg polio, tuberculosis, epilepsy, meningitis, blood disorders, migraine)? If so, please give details.

I sufered from a broken arm when I was four years old

If offered employment, when would you be free to start? after my holiday

Other interests (including sports and hobbies)

Football, Table tenis, Brewing bear

Additional information or relevant experience to support your application

I will work overtime at the weekend

Please indicate in the space below, the name and address of one referee Headmaster Whitworth Comprehensive, Whitworth Rd Manchester

The above information is correct to the best of my knowledge

Signed MR M N JONES Date 31/1/1966

Horseplay

Cast

Foreman: George Stewart
Cost clerk: Rita Bellamy
Apprentice: Steve Gibbs

Scene: A factory paint shop. At 11.05 am on the 16th June George Stewart sees Steve Gibbs limping into the paint shop. Steve is groaning and leaning on Rita, who is taking the weight off his right leg.

George:
What's happened to you?

Rita:
Don't blame him, blame me. We were coming back from the canteen and I slipped on the stairs.

George:
You slipped? But there's only half-a-dozen small steps.

Rita:
I slipped, but Steve made a grab to stop me falling, and he fell instead. I think he's twisted his ankle.

Steve:
It's nothing to worry about, only a sprain. It will get better, I'm sure. Just leave me alone and I'll walk it off.

George:
Take your shoe and sock off. I want to look at this. I can't afford to ignore this. If you fall into a machine in the next half hour, you'll not be the only one in trouble.

George examines Steve's right ankle. It doesn't 'feel' right.

George:
Steve, I'm going to ask Rita to take you to the Accident Hospital in her car. I think it might be a fracture. They will probably do an X-ray, but it's better safe than sorry. I'm going to strap your ankle now with an elastic bandage and give you a couple of aspirins to ease the pain. By the way, you better both tell me exactly what happened.

Steve:
Well it was stupid really. We left the canteen about 11 o'clock and came down the steps into the paint shop as the canteen manageress was coming up the steps with a tray of cups and saucers. I pushed Rita out of the way—only a friendly nudge—you know what I mean—but Rita started to fall. I grabbed her arm, but I slipped and banged into the manageress, who dropped the tray. I slipped down about three steps, feet first to the bottom of the steps. I think I bruised my elbow too. But nobody else was hurt.

George:
(*Examining the elbow*) Yes, you have. I better strap that, just in case. Let's be honest Steve, were you and Rita fooling about? If *you* don't tell me, someone else will. I have to make out an accident report on this, you know.

Steve:
I suppose we were fooling around, but it was very friendly, wasn't it Rita?

Rita:
Yes.

TASK

You are the foreman and you are asked to write an account of the accident on an accident report form (see page 129). Include in your report a diagram depicting the area of the accident (use your imagination for this).

Accident!

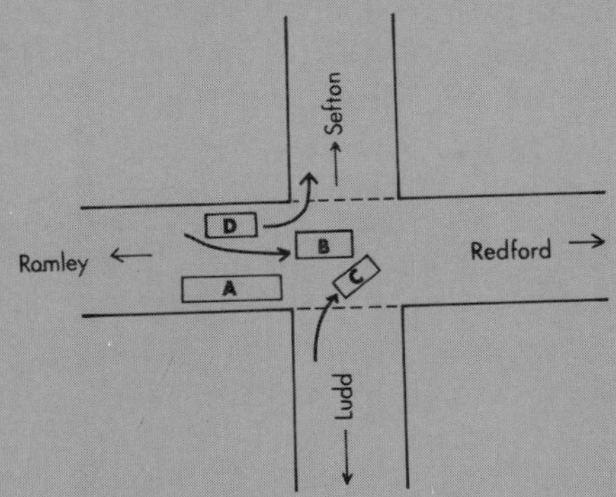

In the diagram, A is a large container lorry which has broken down on its way to Romley (Reg: FDS 438P). The lorry driver has gone to phone for help. B is a Rover 3000 travelling to Redford (Reg: ROB 26S). The driver of the Rover notices that a lorry has broken down but sees a clear road in front of him and increases speed to pass D. D is a Ford Consul (Reg: REB 549V) travelling at a leisurely 30 mph and slowing down to turn left into the road to Sefton. C is a Mini (Reg: FUL 270H) travelling from Ludd to Redford. The Mini has stopped at the road junction and sees a clear road to the right.

Moving forward slowly because the road to the left is obstructed and vision limited, the Mini collides with the Rover which is braking fiercely. Fortunately, the glancing collision does not cause injuries but does result in some damage to both vehicles.

TASK

You are the driver of the Mini and you are claiming damage compensation from your car insurance. When you receive the claim form you realise that there are some questions that need thinking about.

Prepare your answers to the following questions. You may invent details about road and weather conditions, speed restrictions, visibility, vehicle damage, etc, provided the details are reasonably consistent. Please read all the questions before you begin, and do not repeat yourself.

1. Draw an explanatory sketch of the accident, including all vehicles involved either directly or indirectly.
2. Identify each vehicle separately.
3. According to your interpretation, describe the part played in the accident by each vehicle.
4. How did the accident occur?
5. How do you apportion blame? To what degree was each driver to blame for the accident, including yourself?
6. Give details of the extent of injury to persons and damage to vehicles.

Accident report form

Name of injured person: ____________________

Place and time of accident: ____________________

Date: __________

Description of accident:

Diagram in here

Details of accident:

____

Action taken:

____

Completed by: __________ Department: __________

Signature: __________ Date: __________

Job choice

TASK

Using the job application form opposite as a guide, complete the answers it requires in your notebook. You may invent the job title to suit your own preferences and qualifications.

1 Application for CRAFT/TECHNICIAN/OFFICE/OPERATIVE/SALES apprenticeship. (Delete as appropriate)
JOB TITLE

2 SURNAME

3 OTHER NAME(S)

4 DATE OF BIRTH 5 NATIONALITY

6 ADDRESS

7 NAME OF SCHOOLS/COLLEGES ATTENDED TYPE FROM TO

EXAMINATIONS TAKEN (GCE, CSE, etc)

SPECIFY INDIVIDUAL SUBJECTS

THOSE PASSED (include grades if known)

RESULTS AWAITED

8 STATE WITH REGARD TO YOUR LAST OR PRESENT SCHOOL ATTENDED: ADDRESS

FINAL FORM/CLASS FINAL POSITION IN FORM

9 DATE AT WHICH FULL TIME EDUCATION CEASES/CEASED

10 ARE YOU WILLING TO SIT THE COMPANY ENTRANCE EXAMINATION?

11 RESPONSIBILITIES (captain, monitor, prefect, etc)

12 DETAILS OF ANY PREVIOUS JOB EXPERIENCE (holiday employment, part-time work, etc)

13 MEDICAL HISTORY (give particulars)

14 GENERAL INFORMATION (include here any information about yourself not already stated which you feel may be of interest to us in support of your application)

15 STATE, IN A FEW WORDS, WHY YOU WISH TO JOIN THIS COMPANY

16 IF ACCEPTED, ARE YOU PREPARED TO:
(a) JOIN FIRST-AID TRAINING CLASSES?
(b) ATTEND TECHNICAL COLLEGE ON DAY RELEASE?
(c) JOIN A TRADE-UNION?

17 SIGNATURE OF CANDIDATE DATE

18 TO BE SIGNED BY PARENT/GUARDIAN IF APPLICANT IS UNDER 18:
SIGNATURE OF PARENT OR GUARDIAN DATE

19 NAMES AND ADDRESSES OF TWO REFEREES:

City college

TASK

On page 131 is an application form used to enrol students into a college of further education. Enter the information it requires in your notebook. If you are waiting for examination results, include the known details and record the letters AR (Awaiting Results) in the 'Grade' column.

131

TICK CORRECT BOX	SURNAME	[2
MR.	Maiden Name (if Married Women)	[3
MRS. / MISS.	OTHER NAMES	[4

		PERMANENT HOME ADDRESS
AGE AT 1st SEPT.	YRS.	No. & Street [5
DATE OF BIRTH	D M Y	District [6
		Town [7
COUNTRY OF BIRTH		County or Country [8
IF NOT UK STATE DATE OF ENTRY TO UK		Post Code #
		Telephone No.

EMPLOYERS NAME & ADDRESS	ADDRESS WHILE ON COURSE (IF DIFFERENT)
	No. & Street [
	District [
	Town [
	County [
Post Code	Post Code #
Telephone No.	Telephone No.
NATURE OF BUSINESS	DATE OF MOVE TO ABOVE ADDRESS
ARE YOU ATTENDING A SECONDARY SCHOOL FULL TIME YES OR NO____	IF YES GIVE NAME OF SCHOOL

PREVIOUS EDUCATION

DID YOU ATTEND THIS COLLEGE *LAST YEAR?* YES OR NO____	GIVE NAME OF COURSE TAKEN IN *LAST YEAR* AND RESULT (PASS OR FAIL)
IF NOT GIVE NAME AND ADDRESS OF SCHOOL OR COLLEGE, OPEN UNIVERSITY OR CORRESPONDENCE COURSE ATTENDED	
DID YOU ATTEND THIS COLLEGE *PRIOR TO LAST YEAR?* YES OR NO____	IF YES GIVE DATES____ COURSE____

PLEASE GIVE DETAILS BELOW OF ALL EXAMINATION ACHIEVEMENTS TO DATE

NAME & ADDRESS OF SCHOOL OR COLLEGE	EXAMINING BODY	EXAMINATIONS PASSED		GRADE	YEAR
		SUBJECT	STAGE LEVEL		

STUDENT'S SIGNATURE I declare that I have checked the information given in this enrolment form and that to the best of my knowledge it is correct. I agree to abide by College regulations.	DATE

11 Finding out

Often we find ourselves in situations where we have to find out information. We may need to know how to claim a tax rebate or whether a course we want to take is running at the local technical college. There are no easy ways to find out information, but there are some general rules which can make the task a little easier.

Read the following extract and see if you can spot the errors one young worker made in attempting to obtain information about a career in catering:

John went along to the local careers office to obtain information about working in the catering industry. He had done some domestic science at school and he fancied himself as a master chef. When he arrived at the careers office he noticed that the staff were very busy dealing with many young people. After a short wait John was seen by a Mrs Jones:

'Good morning. How can we help you?'

'Well I want to find out about becoming a chef.'

'I see.' Mrs Jones was thumbing through a batch of leaflets. 'You want a career in catering?' She handed him a leaflet.

'I suppose so,' John said, taking the leaflet.

John looked at the leaflet. There was far more to catering than he had imagined.

'You see,' he told Mrs Jones, 'I'd like to travel as well.'

'I see.'

'I wondered if I could get a job cooking abroad?'

'Well it's possible but I think you have to think about basic training first.'

'Oh, I see.' John sounded disappointed. He didn't fancy the idea of having to go to college.

'You see,' Mrs Jones explained, 'there's a lot of different jobs within catering. But if you want to be a chef you have to go to college.'

John wondered if catering was for him after all. He knew how to do a fry-up. He was sure he could pick up things by watching someone doing the job. He thought about the job his cousin Graham had. He was a cook in the army catering corps.

'You see my cousin is a cook in the army. I think I'd really fancy that. He's been all over the world. He was in Georgetown last year. That's in South America.'

'I see.' Mrs Jones thumbed through some more leaflets. 'You might be interested in this then.'

She handed John a leaflet about a career in the army catering corps. He looked at it with interest.

'Shall I fix an appointment for you?'

'Yes please.'

'Right. You've got an appointment this afternoon with a Sgt Morris. I'm sure he'll be able to help you.'

John left the office. He was a little disappointed. Then he realised that he hadn't really thought enough about catering. At least the careers officer had let him into the secret that there was more to catering than meets the eye.

Exercise

John made a number of mistakes which could easily have been avoided. List the mistakes you think he made.

First of all John hadn't really thought enough about what he wanted to do in the catering industry. He was too vague about the type of job he wanted. He thought he could be a chef. But he also wanted to travel. Then he had ideas about a career in the army. When we attempt to 'find out' we should:

- ask ourselves why we want the information
- decide exactly what we want to find out
- be as precise as possible when requesting information. This will help the person to help us
- keep an open mind and be prepared to change our ideas when we receive new information. Often we will be given details that we haven't thought of before

It is always a good idea to jot down a list of questions before you leave home. Try to predict problems and obstacles you are likely to meet. Finding out should be a rewarding and interesting experience.

Try asking

John eventually got a job with a catering firm. All was going well until one Friday when he collected his wages:

'Hey!' he shouted over to his friend Dave. 'How much have you picked up this week?'

'The usual including the overtime,' Dave replied.

'Well I reckon I'm three quid light.'

'Let's have a look. Maybe you've paid more tax.'

Dave came over and looked at John's wage slip.

'I can't see what's happened here—although—hang on a minute—you've got a letter T after your code number.'

'What does that mean?'

'I think it means you've been given a temporary coding.'

'That's wonderful news.' John was saving up to put down a deposit on a new scooter. He wasn't pleased.

'I'll go to the tax office and sort it out. I'm not standing for this.'

John is angry and he isn't thinking clearly. Should he go straight to the tax office or is there another course of action open to him?

He realised that it would be more sensible if he went directly to his firm's wages department. When he got there he spoke to one of the clerks, Mr Fairweather:

'I think I'm short this week in my wages.'

'Well let me have a look at your slip.'

John handed it over and Mr Fairweather looked at it carefully.

'You've been put on a T Coding. I think there's some confusion about how much you earned in that part-time job you did a couple of months ago.'

In an effort to build up his deposit for his scooter John had taken a job in the evening at a local Hamburger bar.

'I thought that had all been sorted out.'

'Well I don't think it has. Why not phone the tax office and see what they can advise? I'll give you their number.'

'I'll do better than that,' said John getting more and more angry, 'I'll go to the tax office this afternoon during the lunch break.'

'What I would do is . . .'

Before he could finish the sentence, John had taken his wages slip and rushed out of the room.

What do we notice about John's behaviour? What mistakes is he making?

First of all he is getting annoyed and he is not thinking straight. He could easily have taken Mr Fairweather's advice and telephoned the tax office. He is being far too hasty. Secondly, the wages clerk is offering him advice—good advice—but John is ignoring it. Don't forget that there are many people who know things that we don't know. We should always be prepared to listen to experts and to make the most of their advice and knowledge.

Later in the afternoon, John was telling Dave about his experience at the tax office.

'You wouldn't believe the number of people down there. It was crazy. There are hundreds of different tax districts all in one building. I didn't know which one was mine.'

'Didn't you know that? You want to think about things a bit more. You get too excited. Didn't you ask Mr Fairweather about it?'

'Well I knew where the place was so when I got there I just went into the first room I saw that was full of people. I thought I had to be in the right place.'

'Why didn't you ask?'

'You don't want to look a fool, do you?'

'No, it's much better to sit there wasting your bloody time.'

'It turned out OK in the end.'

'Yes, but you were late back for work and I had to finish off your job.'

'Anyway I found out that the tax office was waiting to get a form back from the "Burger Palace". I've phoned the Palace and it's all sorted out now.'

Exercise

Read through this section again. Write down what action you think John should have taken.

If you think through a problem first, not only will you know what to ask but also who to ask.

John's case is fairly straightforward. He works for Hilton Catering and he has found that he has less in his wage packet than he expects. His first course of action is to go to his wages department. The clerk there explains that his coding is temporary as the tax office is waiting for a form to be returned from a company John has worked for part-time. John could easily have telephoned the 'Burger Palace' to find out why they had failed to send the appropriate form to the Inland Revenue. He could then have contacted his tax district office by telephone. Mr Fairweather would have been pleased to supply all the details if John hadn't been so eager to rush about wasting everybody's time.

The important point to remember is that if you don't know something, always ask for help. You wouldn't walk about a strange town hoping that you might reach your destination through sheer luck. We all like to be asked questions because it tells us that people think we are capable of helping them. Don't be frightened when you visit unfamiliar places or when you have to meet important people or officials. Generally speaking, people expect you to ask them questions, and this is usually the best way to find out what you want to know.

136 Reading between the lines

Some months later John comes across this advertisement in his local evening paper. While he is happy with his present job, the advertisement intrigues him:

The Manhatten Hotel Group
This fast expanding group is looking for young men and women
with some catering experience
to train in a variety of skills required by the hotel trade.
The Manhatten Hotel Group
has 42 hotels throughout the UK and is also
expanding its operations in parts of Europe and the Middle East.
We will give the right applicants excellent training.

This is a rewarding job with plenty of opportunities and
a first class salary during training and after.
If you are aged between 17 and 23
this could be the post you are looking for.
If you think you could be a first-class expert
then join a hotel group that provides a service that is second to none.

For more information
telephone
Malcolm Harris
on Freephone 96721

John immediately thinks of smart international hotels catering for the rich and famous—even the Jet Set. He decides to telephone Malcolm Harris. What information should he ask for?

John should first of all ask what vacancies exist so he can decide whether it is worth his while pursuing the matter any further. He will want to know about the salary. He may be offered less than his present wage but, after training, his salary may greatly increase. John will also want to know about training. What does this actually involve? Will he get qualifications? Who will pay for this training? He will also be interested in where exactly he will be working. How often will he have to move from one area to another? Will he live in at one of the hotels or will he have to find his own accommodation?

Exercise What other matters will John need to think about?

The lesson to be learnt from this is that information may not always be what it seems. Information can be presented in such a vague way as to be unclear and sometimes misleading . Finding out always means applying our common sense and intelligence to ensure that we are not being led up the garden path.

Information from a library

John has telephoned Malcolm Harris at the Manhatten and has arranged an informal interview where many questions can be dealt with. John is aware that he knows little about careers in the hotel industry and feels that it would be useful to find out more before he commits himself. He decides to visit his local library to see if there are any books on the subject.

The last time John went to a library he was still at school. But this library was slightly different. It seemed less threatening and there were more interesting things to look at.

'Hello, I'd like to join the library,' he said to the girl at the desk marked 'Enquiries'.

'That's easy. All you have to do is to fill in this form. Then I can give you your library tickets and a printed guide to the library. If you want me to help you with anything afterwards, just ask.'

John completed the form filling and sat down to read the guide. It explained that the non-fiction (factual) books were kept on shelves in number order according to something called the *Dewey Classification Scheme*.

The guide had a list of the main classes of Dewey:

000 GENERAL WORKS	500 PURE SCIENCE
100 PHILOSOPHY	600 TECHNOLOGY
200 RELIGION	700 ARTS & RECREATION
300 SOCIAL SCIENCES	800 LITERATURE
400 LANGUAGES	900 HISTORY

John wandered around the library. He felt confused by the number of books stacked high on the shelves. He picked one up—it was about water cycle maintenance. He wondered what that was. There was another shelf packed with enormous encyclopaedias.

He felt confused and returned to the enquiry desk. 'Excuse me, I'm trying to find the books about the hotel trade. I've looked in the guide but I can't find any information about where they're kept.'

'Don't forget that the booklet is only a general guide. What exactly are you looking for?'

'Well, I was looking for a book on hotel catering as a career.'

'Come with me,' she said, walking towards a large wooden unit marked *Library Catalogue*. She went to the section marked *Subject Index*, pulled out a drawer and fingered through a pile of cards. She explained to John that the subject index listed the Dewey numbers for all the non-fiction books in the library.

'If you look at the card headed HOTELS, you can see all the numbers of the different aspects of hotel work in the library's book stock.'

John looked at the card.

HOTELS	
ACCOUNTING	657.837
BUILDINGS	728.5
CAREERS	338.4764
COOKERY	641.572
MANAGEMENT	647.94
RECEPTION DUTIES	647.6

'There you are,' the librarian said, eventually handing John a couple of books to look at. 'You see the best way of finding out about what books we have is to have a good look round. Get to know the library. Next month we are replacing the index cards with a microcomputer, but the system of finding books will be the same as it is now.'

John decided that he would spend some time looking at the different shelves in order to get to know where everything was.

'You've chosen an interesting career,' the librarian commented, 'working in the hotel industry. All those opportunities for travel about the country and abroad of course.'

'I don't know about that. I don't know any foreign languages.'

'Well you could always take out a set of records from the *Record Lending* section. They've got whole language courses for beginners for loan.'

'Records?' John said sounding surprised.

'Yes. You can borrow records. And don't think it's only classical and educational ones. We have plenty of jazz and pop records too.'

'I didn't know that.'

'As I told you,' the librarian said as she walked away, 'there's more to libraries than just books. You have a look for yourself and you'll see what I mean.'

Plan of library

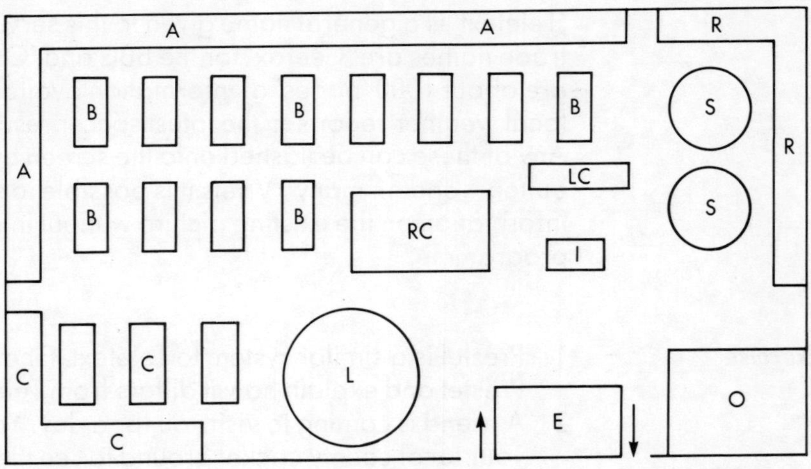

A = Adult fiction arranged in author alphabetical order.
B = Adult non-fiction in Dewey number order.
C = Children's books.
L = Lounge area with soft chairs. Newspapers and magazine rack.
RC = Record and cassette library: classical records, pop, jazz, folk, language tapes and cassettes, books on cassette, video cassettes, etc.
LC = Library catalogue or computerised book-finding facility.
I = Information desk for readers' enquiries. Member of staff always available.
R = Reference books, telephone directories, maps, encyclopedias.
S = Study chairs and tables.
O = Library office. Photocopying service available for small charge.
E = Entrance and exit with electronic alarm security system, and staffed counters for return and issue of books.

John decided to follow this advice. He turned to the booklet and found a diagram showing a layout of the library (above).

Electronic information

When Archie woke he realised that he was going to miss the 0915 train. He had overslept again. He rushed downstairs and turned on the TV and pressed the digits 100 on a remote-control handset. Right, he thought, let's see if there is any information about the train service into town.

Looking at the TV set he saw the word 'Index' at the top of the screen. Halfway down he read 'Travel—Rail—Page 287'. Archie punched these numbers on his handset and got his answer—all trains had been delayed by up to 50 minutes because of urgent repairs to the track. He hadn't missed his train after all.

Even if you are not familiar with the 'Teletext' system, you can see how it is possible to find out all kinds of things without ever getting out of the armchair!

What is Teletext?

Teletext is a free service broadcast by the BBC and ITV which provides all kinds of up-to-date information and entertainment on some TV sets (they are usually more expensive). The word 'Teletext' is a general name given to this service, but the actual trade names are 'Ceefax' for the BBC and 'Oracle' for ITV. There are about 1000 'pages' of information available, varying from local weather reports to the latest soccer results and film reviews. Any of these can be flashed onto the screen by pressing a button—and on many TV sets it is possible to superimpose the information on the existing picture without interrupting the normal programme.

Exercise

1 Prestel is a similar system to Teletext. Find out more about Prestel and explain how it differs from Teletext.

2 A friend is coming to visit you for a day. You plan to travel to your local county cricket ground to see the third day of a match between the county side and a visiting team of West Indian All Stars. Before your friend arrives you decide to plan the day so that everything will run smoothly.

You have access to a Teletext service. What kind of information will you be able to extract from the Teletext service that will help you both to enjoy a successful and trouble-free day?

Tips on finding out

1 **For most people, finding out means asking the right questions of the right people. Next time you have a problem or a query think hard about who is the best person to go to for help or information.**

2 **If you aren't sure who to go to for advice, then ask someone you respect for help first. Ask them where *they* would go to get the best advice.**

3 **If you need specialist help or you intend to buy something, say a second-hand car or a bike, it really does pay to shop around to find out all you can before you spend your money. Always take an expert with you to advise you about mechanical or electrical second-hand goods.**

4 **If finding out means going to a government office to meet an official, first think through the questions you want answered. Sensible people jot down their questions on paper.**

5 **Sometimes you may find obstacles blocking your path to finding things out. Don't lose your temper and don't give up too easily. If you are prepared to make just a little nuisance of yourself you will be surprised how much you can find out by sticking to your guns.**

6 **Be prepared to use libraries and their facilities. They are very interesting places once you know your way around. Librarians, too, are always keen to help anyone in trouble.**

Local sports

Geoff set off to his friend's house to watch TV. When he arrived Pete was already engrossed in a programme about hang gliding.

'Sit down and watch this. It's really interesting.'

Geoff sat down and watched the programme. He had to agree with Pete. The programme was interesting. He fancied the idea of hang gliding himself.

'I'd really like to have a go at that,' said Pete, switching to another channel at the end of the programme.

'Yes, I know what you mean. But the trouble with this town is that there's no chance of doing anything like that. If you don't play football you've had it.'

'Yes, I suppose you're right.'

Pete and Geoff settled down to another night's telly.

Geoff and Pete have given up without really trying to find out if any organisation is involved with hang gliding in their town. This often happens. People give up without really trying to find out. Most of us would be surprised to discover the number of sporting and leisure activities catered for in most areas.

TASK

You want to find out what sporting and leisure activities are catered for in your locality. First of all, think about how you intend to seek out this information and then jot down your ideas on paper. For example, asking all your friends what they know might be one source of information. Make a complete list of sources of information.

The second part of the task is to produce a list of names, addresses and phone numbers of sporting and leisure organisations in your locality.

Wedding plans

142

John was on his way to work when he met up with an old friend, Tony.

'Long time no see,' John greeted his mate.

'Hello John. It has been a long time. I've been busy with this and that.'

'Oh yes,' John replied, wondering if Tony would confirm or deny the rumour that Tony was getting married.

'I suppose you've heard the good news then?'

'Good news?' John replied, grinning. He was keeping his cards close to his chest.

'Come off it John, I'm sure you've heard about me getting spliced.'

'Oh I might have heard something.'

'In three weeks in fact.'

'What about an invitation then?'

Tony explained that John would be getting his invitation soon. Sandra, his fiancée, was looking after that side of things. Tony explained that there were a hundred and one jobs to do. Getting married was a complicated business.

The two friends parted, having arranged to meet in the evening for a quick drink. As John headed off to work he thought again about all the jobs Tony said he'd had to do in arranging his marriage. He tried to think what had to be done . . . his own wedding wasn't that far off.

TASK

In your notebook draw three columns under the following headings. Complete the left-hand column first. Completing the other two columns will take some careful thought and research.

Demon drink!

TASK

You are to produce a two-page A4 leaflet informing and warning young people of the possible dangers associated with the consumption of alcohol. Your leaflet must include the following two boxed illustrations. You will need to find out as much information as possible on the subject from any available source. These illustrations were obtained from the Health Education Council.

Draw same-sized rectangles to indicate the position of the illustrations on your leaflet.

Wedding arrangements		
What is to be done?	Where to get information	Questions to ask

Percentage alcohol levels of different drinks

In terms of the concentration of absolute alcohol, the relative order of strength is: 1 spirits, 2 fortified wines, 3 table wines, 4 beer

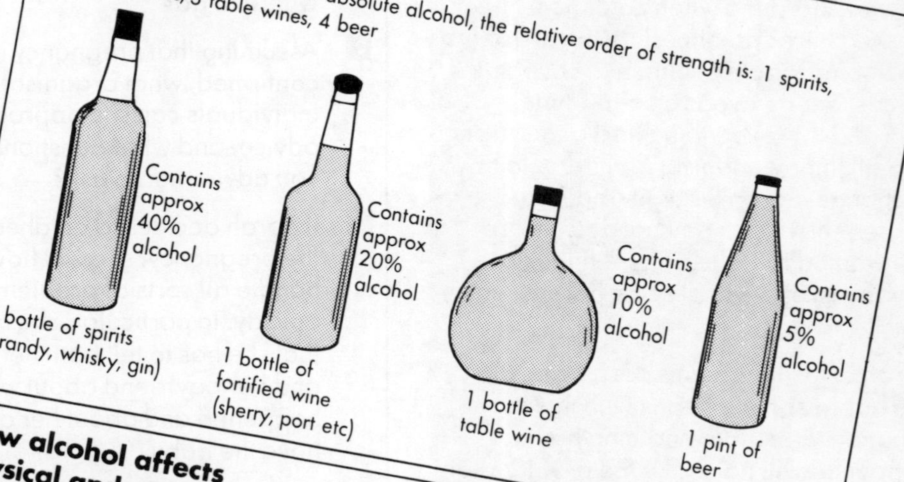

How alcohol affects physical and mental behaviour

As soon as alcohol enters the bloodstream it begins to affect judgment, self-control and skills, including driving. It is not possible to predict precisely how everyone will be affected, since it depends on the amount drunk and the personality of the individual, but the chart below gives an indication of the kind of effects which might be expected:

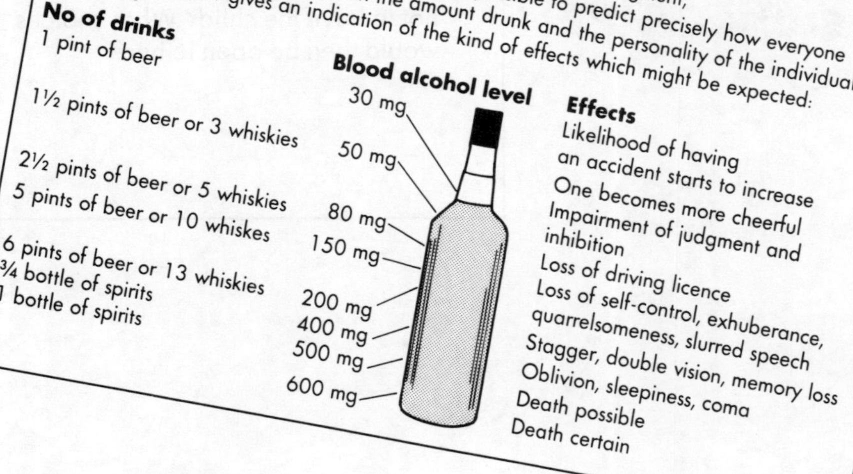

Baby talk

144 Sarah was heartbroken. It had occurred to her that she was probably pregnant. Strange, she thought, how one minute you are on top of the world and the next minute everything has gone hopelessly wrong. Only three weeks ago she and Peter had announced their engagement. They had decided that they would marry in two years' time when Peter had finished his apprenticeship. Sarah for the time being would continue at college for at least another year on a full-time course. Now everything had gone wrong and all their wonderful plans would have to change. Sarah thought about the future—having to get married before she wanted to—the baby—financial problems. She wondered what she was going to do.

Sarah's position seems desperate. But she has to come to terms with this new situation. Pretending nothing has happened will not make the problems go away.

TASK
(working in a small discussion group with one person taking notes)

Think about what Sarah ought to do now. Obviously there are things that should be done before anything else, such as seeking medical advice.

1. Where can Sarah go or how can she find out whether or not she is really pregnant? Are there any advantages or disadvantages to consider in making a choice about where to go?
2. Assuming that pregnancy is confirmed, what organisations or individuals can she approach for advice, and what questions would you advise her to ask?
3. If Sarah decides to go ahead with the pregnancy, she will have to handle all sorts of problems fairly quickly. In particular, she might feel that she has to tell both her parents and her boyfriend about what has happened and about her decision to have the baby.

   What advice would you give Sarah about the best way to handle this? What should she do if either her parents or her boyfriend wishes her not to have the child? What choices would then be open to her?

4 If and when the baby is to be born, many practical problems will have to be dealt with. Find out, through discussion, thinking about it for yourself and researching the subject, as much as you can about what Sarah ought to know and to do about:

- attending college
- where to live or type of accommodation required
- social security benefits and welfare
- child benefits and maternity grants
- needs of the child in the first three months.

Jot down as much information and advice as you can on all these matters, including any problems that might arise. You might find it useful to share the workload for this question.

When you have finished this task, make sure that your notes are in proper order. You may be asked to give a short oral report on this subject.

Windfall

145

Martin received some good news in the post. It was a letter from a solicitor in Bristol. An unknown aunt had died recently and Martin had been left £2500 in her will. As he was about to be married in 18 months' time, Martin decided that the best plan would be to invest the money and make some interest. Martin knew nothing at all about investment. He had heard that people put money in the post office, but the more he thought about it the more the idea of finding the best investment appealed to him.

TASK

Where should Martin go for advice? Make a list of possible places Martin could go for information, and find out for yourself what would be the safest and most profitable investment for his windfall.

Gone missing

Simon went babysitting with his girlfriend. Everything went well until two days later he received a letter from the child's father. The letter accused Simon of taking 20 pounds from a drawer in the house when the parents were out. Simon knew this was nonsense, but he was worried about the accusation. The letter went on to say that if he didn't pay the money back within a week the police would be contacted. He felt it was wrong that he should be forced to pay back the money he hadn't taken. He wondered what the best course of action would be.

TASK

Where do you think Simon should go for the best advice on this matter? What questions should he ask when he gets there?

Crisis!

When Richard came home from work, his mother told him the bad news. His father's medical condition had deteriorated and the doctors had told her to expect the worst. His mother was deeply upset. His father had already been in hospital for over a month and money was running short. His mother had just received a final demand from the Electricity Board and the Rates demand was due at any time. The last thing Richard wanted on his mother's mind was the worry over finance. He told her to leave everything to him. He would try to sort things out.

After his dinner, Richard sat down with a sheet of paper and began to make a list of all the things he would have to look into.

TASK
(working in a small group)

What type of household expenditure will Richard have to take into account?

Make a list of their most immediate problems. What would you do and where would you go for advice if this sort of financial crisis happened in your family? Are there any other things that a person can do to help themselves in this sort of situation?

Getting about

- 'What I don't like is the way I'm forced to depend on people. I have difficulty walking, but if I take things slowly I can manage. But when I go into the town centre, well, there's all those subways and stairs. You just can't get about.'
- 'I take my mother from time to time into the town centre. She's confined to a wheelchair. Well, it's almost impossible to get her about. I know people like my mother are in a minority . . . but you would think that some provision could be made.'
- 'I bet the fella who planned the centre of this town had two good legs.'

(These quotes are taken from people interviewed on a local BBC radio programme.)

A lot of people now believe that town planners should give more thought to the needs of the disabled. The centres of our towns and cities are not, at the best of times, ideal places for the disabled.

This exercise has been designed to give you the opportunity of finding out at first hand the difficulties faced by disabled people in our community.

TASK
(working in small groups)

The object of the task is to find out as much as you can about the problems disabled people face in a particular building, or group of buildings, or area, in the town centre.

Each group should first decide which part of the town it intends to visit to research the problem. It might be a department store, library or a railway station. *The task will be completed when a set of notes and supporting diagrams are produced detailing the difficulties a disabled person would experience in a wheelchair.* The information will be presented as a wall display.

It is entirely a matter for each group how it intends to conduct its research. Obviously, there is no substitute for a real wheelchair and a volunteer! The following headings and notes are offered for consideration only:

- *Entrances and exits*—Are the doors wide enough? Are there difficult steps?
- *Information display*—Are there any signs to help and guide the disabled?
- *Counters and tills*—Are they too low or high? Are they accessible?
- *Gangways*—Are they wide enough? Are there any obstacles?
- *Toilets*—Are special toilets provided? Can they be reached?
- *Stairs and lifts*—Are lifts available? Are the buttons too high?
- *Staff attitudes*—Are the staff willing to help? Are they welcoming?

When you have gathered the information you are ready to begin the wall display.

The library

148 *The tasks on these two pages are meant to be carried out in a public or a college/school library. Students should be guided by a tutor or a librarian in the initial stages.*

TASK

Look at the Dewey Classification System on page 149 and, with the help of a dictionary, explain simply the meaning of:

- Commerce
- Technology
- Recreation
- Literature
- Zoology
- Geology
- Philosophy

TASK

When you are familiar with the library's reference system, make a list of the titles of two books on each of the following subjects:

- Computers
- The Second World War
- Safety at work
- Humour
- Swimming

Present your information under the following headings:

Subject and title	*Author*	*Publisher*	*Date published*	*Library reference number*

TASK

Look at the Dewey chart again. Under which subject heading and reference number (there may be more than one) would you find information on the following topics?

- Power gliding
- History of England
- Learning French
- Taking photographs
- World population
- The handicapped
- Life on other planets
- Microelectronics in the office

TASK

Find the following books in the reference section and make notes on the type of information they contain:

Guinness Book of Records
Who's Who?
Whitaker's Almanack
Chambers' Technical Dictionary

The Dewey Classification System

000 GENERAL WORKS
010 Bibliography
020 Library science
030 General cyclopaedias
040 General collections
050 General periodicals
060 General Societies Museums
070 Journalism
080 Collected works
090 Book rarities

100 PHILOSOPHY
110 Metaphysics
120 Metaphysical theories
130 Fields of psychology
140 Specific philosophical viewpoints
150 Psychology
160 Logic
170 Ethics
180 Ancient philosophy
190 Modern philosophy

200 RELIGION
210 Natural theology
220 Bible
230 Doctrinal theology
240 Devotional theology
250 Pastoral theology
260 Ecclesiastical theology
270 Christian church history
280 Christian churches and sects
290 Non-Christian religions

300 SOCIAL SCIENCES
310 Statistics
320 Political science
330 Economics
340 Law
350 Public administration
360 Social welfare
370 Education
380 Commerce
390 Customs

400 LANGUAGES
410 Comparative
420 English language
430 German Germanic
440 French Provençal
450 Italian Rumanian
460 Spanish Portuguese
470 Latin Other Italic
480 Greek Hellenic group
490 Other languages

500 PURE SCIENCE
510 Mathematics
520 Astronomy
530 Physics
540 Chemistry
550 Geology
560 Palaeontology
570 Biology
580 Botany
590 Zoology

600 TECHNOLOGY
610 Medicinal sciences
620 Engineering
630 Agriculture
640 Domestic economy
650 Commerce
660 Chemical technology
670 Manufactures
680 Manufactures (continued)
690 Building construction

700 ARTS and RECREATIONS
710 Landscape architecture
720 Architecture
730 Sculpture
740 Drawing Decoration Art
750 Painting
760 Engraving
770 Photography
780 Music
790 Recreation

800 LITERATURE
810 American
820 English
830 German Germanic
840 French Provençal
850 Italian Rumanian
860 Spanish Portuguese
870 Latin Other Italic
880 Greek Hellenic group
890 Other languages

900 HISTORY
910 Geography
920 Biography
930 Ancient world history
940 Europe
950 Asia
960 Africa
970 N America
980 S America
990 Oceania and polar regions

12 Photographs, illustrations and posters

Photographs and illustrations are often used effectively to convey information and ideas. In certain circumstances they are an ideal method of communication because so much of what we learn results from what we see. If you had to describe in writing what your face looked like, for instance, can you imagine how difficult it would be? Or if you tried to describe orally the shape of a paper clip without the help of a sketch, do you think that you could manage it? Obviously, photographs and illustrations have their uses!

Photographs

One of the more common uses of the photograph is the personal or group photograph. How many times have you been part of this kind of conversation?

Jimmy: You should have been with us. You'd have had a great time.

Colin: I wish I had been. It was one of those things. Maybe I'll make it next year. I've never been to the Blackpool Illuminations.

Jimmy: You should have seen Kenny. He's a real joker. Have a look at this photo. Look at Colin. He's a clown at times. Jenny's great too.

Colin: I see what you mean. Did he go around like that all day? He really looks like he's having a good time.

Colin sums up the power of the photograph in his last comment. The old saying still holds true—a picture is better than a thousand words. This is because photographs can give an added dimension to communication. Read the following paragraph which came at the end of a short newspaper article and then compare your understanding and interpretation of the written account with the photograph on page 151.

The Kleber wheel is nearly 2 metres in diameter. It is so large that a young lad can easily sit inside it with lots of room to spare! The 'monster' wheel is attached to a gigantic farm machine which was displayed at the Royal Show last Wednesday and formed part of the agricultural machinery display. Things will never be the same down on the farm again. Not with the giant new machinery and those big wheels.

While the writer makes a brave attempt to convey the size of the wheel, his words haven't the impact of the photograph. The writer uses words like 'big' and 'monster' and 'giant' and tries to stir our imagination by asking us to think of a young boy sitting inside the hub-wheel. But it is the photograph which really gets the message across. If we had ideas to visit the Royal Show it is the photograph that would get us there.

Look at the photograph again. Why is it so effective?

Not only can we see the young lad inside the wheel-hub but in the background we can see a man scratching his head, and we can assess the size of the wheel in relation to him.

Look at the man in the background. How would you describe him?

He could easily be saying to himself: 'Am I seeing things, or is that really a wheel?' He looks a little surprised. This is how we might react if we were in his position. The photograph is inviting us to join in, to make comparisons for ourselves. We try to imagine what the actual machine must look like. Our imagination is helped by the shape of the photograph itself. The tall shape increases our awareness of height—of the enormity of the vehicle. Taking everything into account, the information contained in the photograph adds up to a very powerful image.

Reading photographs

Just as we have to learn how to read newspaper articles and instruction booklets effectively, we have to learn to 'read' photographs. Often there is far more information contained in a photograph than we first imagine.

Exercise

Look at the photograph opposite and write down all the facts it contains and any other items of interesting information.

We can see that it is a photograph of a cinema or a 'Picture Palace'. But there is more to it than that. For example:

- The cinema is called 'Talkies'. This tells us that this photograph dates back to a time when 'talking pictures' were new. As with statistical tables and graphs, we can make intelligent guesses or draw conclusions from photographs.
- The films on show are 'The Lottery Bride' and 'The Wrong Mr Perkins'.
- Compared with many modern cinemas, this 'Picture Palace' is very large. It was built at a time before TV and video when the cinema was in its heyday.
- Such were the crowds that the cinemas would employ commissionaires to supervise the large queues. There appear

to be two of them standing at the top of the steps. There is a young lad standing by the door. What was his job?

- The manager of the 'Picture Palace' stands proudly with his staff, who appear to be standing to attention. Are they ex-soldiers perhaps?
- A car is allowed to park in front of the cinema. Were there fewer parking restrictions then?
- The bus stop tells us that the cinema is probably sited on a main road.
- From the name of the cinema and the type of car in the foreground we can get a good idea when the photograph was taken. What year would you say this picture was taken? In what country is the cinema located?

Interpreting photographs

When we look at photographs for the first time we are often struck by their impact and we know that if we look carefully at them we can gain a lot of interesting information. However, we should be aware that such is the power of the photographic image that often we can make different interpretations of the same photograph. Some less reputable newspapers might use a photograph of a crowd scene at a football match, for instance, to suggest a rioting mob simply by changing the camera angle to get a more exciting shot or by feeding in the suggestion in a caption printed beneath the photograph.

We are all guilty of using the camera in this kind of way. As photographers we like to get our victims to 'smile' when they don't want to or to wear funny hats or act the fool. When we are being photographed ourselves we sometimes try to put over our 'best side' and we are always tempted to show our friends the best (meaning the most flattering) photos of ourselves, and discard the less flattering ones. Photographs, like the printed word and the words we use in conversation, are often true, sometimes only half-true and occasionally untrue!

We should always be on our guard against being taken in by the photograph.

Exercise

Look carefully at the photograph opposite. Write a short article of about 100 words to accompany the photograph. Make up a headline first, and using your imagination write an interesting story, including as much information as you can extract from the photograph.

Illustrations

There are many different ways of using illustrations but we often find them used with accompanying words. Illustrations, like photographs, can help us to communicate more effectively. Look at the following illustration and write down the message it is trying to convey:

The illustration is trying to get over the point that smoking can be both irritating and unpleasant for the non-smoker, especially in public places like restaurants. The organisation who have produced this illustration have made their point in this way so that people can 'see' how unpleasant smoking can be. If they had produced a leaflet which read like this, the point would lose impact:

> Some people find cigarette smoke very unpleasant. This is especially true in public places like restaurants.

Now while these words do communicate an important point, the illustration allows the reader to see and imagine for himself the point being made. It also hints at the possibility of the non-smokers taking defensive action against the smokers by complaining to the waiter.

Exercise

You want to illustrate the dangers of overloading an electrical power point. Draw or write down what you should include in your illustration. Ask yourself two questions: am I getting the content of my message across and does the illustration have a powerful impact?

Making things clear

When we buy something, especially a mechanical device, we often find that we are given some form of printed instructions on how to use or assemble the item. The manufacturers will have given some thought on how to make the operating or assembly instructions as clear as possible. The instructions have to be easily understood because the purchaser is involved in a form of one-way communication. You cannot ask questions of the manufacturer once you have taken the product home.

Look at the following example of instructions given away with a *Rightsound* radio:

> The large knob on the far left-hand side of the radio is the tuner control. The first button on the top left is for long wave and next to that is the medium wave button, followed by the FM and tone control buttons. The large button on the top right is the On/Off button, and the pull-up aerial lies across the top. The volume control is the large knob on the right-hand side. When you are having interference, pull up the aerial for improved reception. At the back of the radio you will find the battery hatch. You will require four HP 2 batteries. Good listening. We are sure you will find the 'right sound' on *Rightsound*.

The information given here is ample in terms of explaining to the user how to operate the set. But the way the information is given is dull and more importantly it is an example of ineffective communication.

Why is this?

One problem is that you have to look at the illustration, then at the instructions, then back to the illustration, and so on. Even the way the written instructions are presented is clumsy and not too easy to follow.

Exercise

Using the existing illustration, or an improved version drawn by yourself, how would you improve the operating instructions for the *Rightsound* radio?

It has already been suggested that when giving illustrated instructions we should make each step as clear as possible. Sometimes in our efforts for simplicity we tend to leave things out. Your reworked instruction for the radio could be a case in point. Think about it. What questions could the user ask about the information you have given? List some questions. They might include:

- What exactly is meant by 'long-wave', 'medium-wave' and 'FM'?
- On which wavelength can we find our local radio stations?

Can you think of any more questions to add to this list?

We should keep in mind when we give or receive instructions with items like radios and cassette recorders that we are dealing with *basic* operating instructions only and if someone wants more information they will have to discover it for themselves. With the radio it is a simple matter of turning the set on and moving the tuning control along the wavebands. Sometimes, however, we will find ourselves wanting *exact* information.

Imagine you are having trouble with one of your taps at home. You go along to a Do-It-Yourself shop and ask the shop assistant how a tap works. This is the answer you get:

> 'Well, that's easy. Taps are made up of different parts. You've got your cross head, usually there's a hexagonal gland nut, a jumper plate, and let me see. . . . Ah yes we mustn't forget the good old washer—they often cause all the trouble. Then there's a spindle and a hexagonal nut head.'

After all this you are bound to be confused, and you probably never imagined that a tap was so complicated. What has made life difficult for us is the way the information was presented. There is nothing wrong with the shop assistant's explanation, but unless you know something about taps none of it makes much sense. It would be much simpler if the assistant could show us an illustration such as:

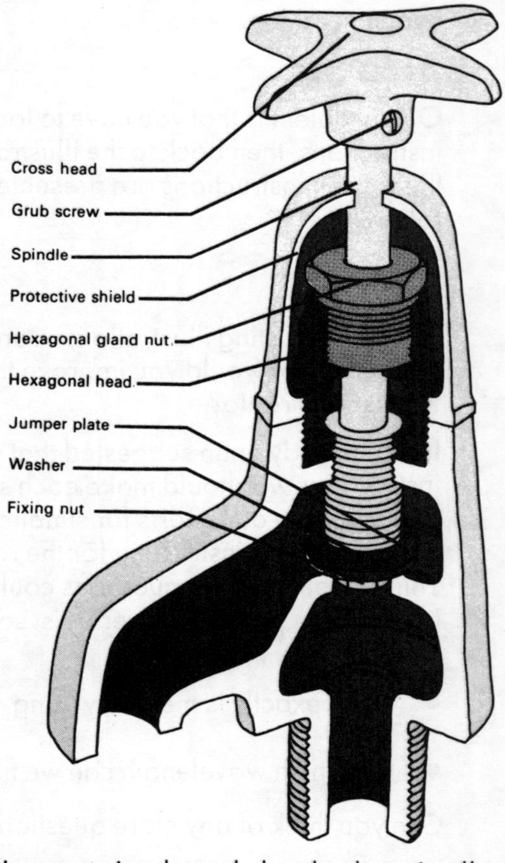

In this illustration, put simply and clearly, there is all you need to know about the parts that make up a tap. To reinforce this information you could check each illustrated part with a tap at home.

Now supposing you want to change the washer. What do you do? You can see where the washer is located from the illustration, but you will require further guidance.

Exercise Here are six illustrations showing the correct sequence in fitting a new tap washer. Beneath, the accompanying word descriptions have been mixed up. Which description fits which illustration?

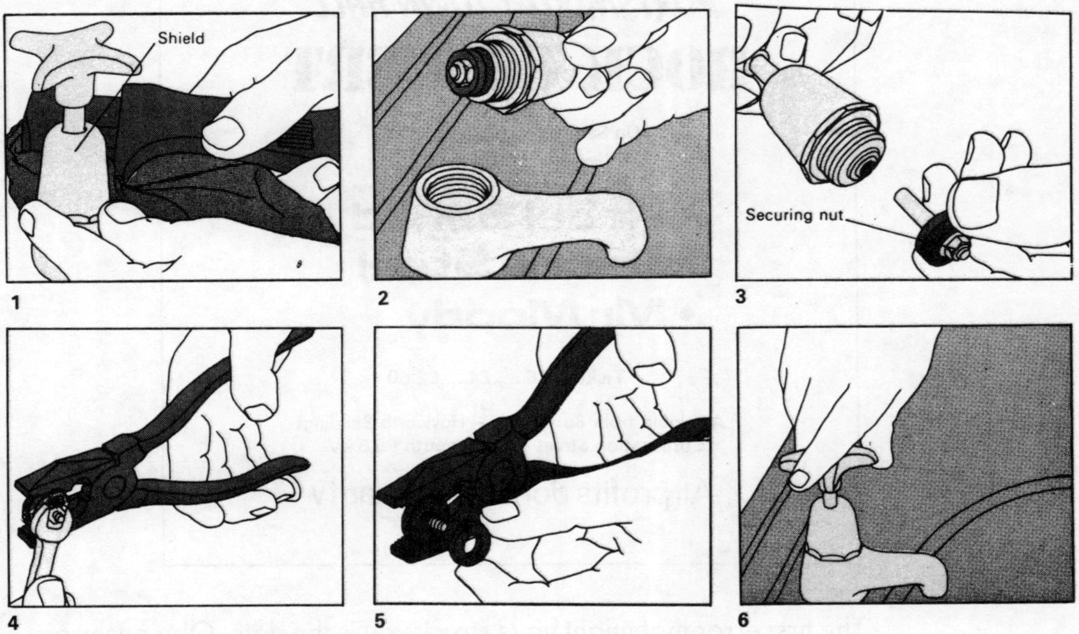

1 With either kind of tap, grip the edge of the jumper plate with pliers. If the washer is held by a nut, undo it with a small spanner.

2 Secure the washer with the nut. Reassemble the tap. Turn on the water supply. Turn the tap on and off to check that it does not drip.

3 Shut off the water supply and open the tap or valve fully. Fit the waste plug in the sink. Protect the shield with a rag and remove it with a spanner.

4 On some taps the jumper can be removed; on others it fits loosely. The washer is usually held against the jumper plate with a small nut.

5 Remove the old washer and fit a matching new one. Fit the inside of the washer bearing the maker's name so that it faces downwards.

6 Loosen the hexagonal head with an adjustable spanner. Unscrew the loosened nut by hand and lift the top of the tap away from the body.

Posters

Look at this poster. Can you spot any errors?

PORTSMOUTH TOWN HALL

ROCK CONCERT

On Saturday 31st September

Three great bands

- **Rebel Sound**
- **Brittle Steel**
- **Mr Moody**

Tickets £5......£4.....£2.50

Available from Box Office – Hayworth Buildings
Corporation Street – Portsmouth P5 6AV

All profits donated to charity

The first error that might have struck you is the date. Obviously, as there are only 30 days in September this date must be wrong. The time of the concert is also missing. We can assume that it might start in the early evening, but we can't be sure. Nor can we be sure of the address of the Town Hall. The organisers might think that everybody knows the whereabouts of the Town Hall, but people travelling from outside Portsmouth may not have a clue. Nor can we assume that the address at the bottom of the poster is the address of the Town Hall. All in all, not a very effective example of visual communication!

Planning the poster

The first point to make about poster making is the need for thinking and planning *before* the design is started. No matter how brilliant you are at drawing or designing, if the words on the poster are wrong or missing, time spent on making it look beautiful is time wasted and could result in total disaster. Just imagine what would happen if fans turned up on the wrong day for a big Rock concert!

So, if you are writing the words for a poster you must decide what information to include and what you intend to exclude. If you leave out valuable information, this could be fatal. If you put in too much, the poster might be so boring that it will be ignored. The skill is to convey the maximum amount of information with the minimum number of words in the most striking way possible.

As a basic guide you should keep in mind what we might call the 'Rule of the five W's'. These are:

- **what** = What is the event or the occasion? (rock concert)
- **when** = When does it take place? (date and time)
- **who** = Who is involved? (name of organisers, artistes, etc)
- **where** = Where is it all happening? (town hall)
- **why** = Does the event have a special meaning? (proceeds to charity)

This rule should help you to ensure that you don't forget something crucial, and it leaves you free to include whatever else you wish.

Exercise Rewrite and correct the wording in the rock concert poster in the previous example. You can invent missing details as required.

Designing the poster

When you know the words are right, and not before, you can start your design. The first thing to think about is the paper. What sheet size do you need? Do you want the paper white or coloured? What shape do you want your poster to be? You can have, say, the traditional shape or a long and thin type which can be pinned in an upright or a lying down position. You can have an unusual shape like a 50 pence coin or a triangle. Unless you are confident of your ability, it might be easier to stick to the usual rectangular shape.

The second requirement is to work out the size and position of the lettering. It is absolutely *essential* to work out some rough designs on a separate sheet first. Professional designers might draw about half-a-dozen different small drawings called 'thumbnail sketches'. Once they know which design to use they draw a full-size rough design to get some idea of what the finished product will look like.

However, whether you are a professional or a complete beginner, your job is to understand what the poster is meant to communicate, and to use your skill and imagination to get the message across effectively. So study the words carefully. What are the really important words? What is the most effective way to display them—big letters, strong colours? What design style is best suited for the occasion? Where on the sheet should we position our important and our less important information?

Lastly, the design itself. Keep two things in mind:

- Is my design *original and striking* enough to catch the eye and to stop people in their tracks to look at it?
- When they do stop, can they *understand* what my poster is trying to communicate?

Exercise Using the corrected words of the previous exercise, design a poster of striking visual impact.

Tips on visual communication

1. If you have something to communicate, always consider the possibility of using photographs or illustrations to convey the information.
2. It is possible for the camera to lie. Be prepared to be critical of photographs that appear in newspapers.
3. Draw illustrations as clearly as you can. *Don't* clutter up drawings with unnecessary detail. Use a coding device such as letters or colours to identify important features in the accompanying written descriptions.
4. Always label your drawings accurately.
5. With posters, take as much time as you need to get the words right before you start your design.
6. Remember that the parts of the poster left empty, such as the space on each side of lines of words, are an important part of the design. *Don't* think that you have to cover the whole sheet with lettering or designs. Use space to emphasise important lines of words.
7. *Don't* sacrifice effective communication by being too flashy with your designs. Good designers aim to improve the quality of the communication.

Ideas in focus

Top teenage magazine photographer, Adrian Rickenbecker, has been given a tough assignment: to produce a set of photographs on 'Young fashion in the 1980s'.

He remembered his first job as a features photographer five years ago. He was sent out to photograph 'People and their pets'. He walked for miles looking for a man with a dog. All he got for his trouble was a good soaking in the rain.

Rickenbecker knows now that planning ahead is the smart thing to do. First, he thought, he will get some ideas on paper.

Fashion in the 1980s – ideas

- Talk to anyone who knows anything about the subject. Is there anybody I know personally who could help?
- Go to the local art college to talk to fashion design teachers and students. Ask if the students are prepared to model their own designs. Would they model other clothes too? Smart thinking!
- Go to fashion boutiques in town. Ask what the young people are buying. Ask for permission to take photographs. Could ask if clothes could be hired – maybe get art students to model them on the premises.
- Go to the reference library. Ask about recent books and mags on the subject.
- Go to the 'Rebel Sound' concert on Saturday night. Could photo willing fans who are wearing something interesting? Check disco/gigs in town. Could local radio help?
- Spend time in the shopping centre on Saturday morning. Could bump into some trendy dressers!
- Must cover the whole range of fashion – punks, romantics, rainbow heads, school-girl look, head bangers, teds and bikers, etc. Equal sex treatment.
- Could develop a theme here? Revival v. Modern or 'Is there such a thing as unisex fashion?'

There's nothing like getting ideas down on paper, Rickenbecker thought. I've got a few useful things to think about now, and it's only taken me a few minutes.

TASK

Imagine that you are a photographer working for the same organisation. Make out a list of ideas on a topic chosen by yourself. Here are some ideas to get you started:

- Where do the unemployed youth spend their time?
- Danger at work.
- Hair styles for teenagers.
- Interesting places to visit in this area.
- Make-up for men.
- How safe are pedestrianised shopping areas?
- The teenage alcoholic.
- Local bands.

If you have a camera, you might like to try out some of your ideas 'for real'. You could write captions for your best photographs to produce an interesting visual project. If you have access to video camera equipment and playback, then try making a short programme based on your ideas.

Road safety campaign

164

As part of a road safety campaign, the Ministry of Transport decides to produce a handout to promote sensible driving.

On A4 design a suitable poster or handout that would persuade drivers that careful driving is good driving. Decide on your wording *before* you begin your design. You must include the following photograph as an illustration. Draw a same-size rectangle to indicate the position of the photograph on your poster.

The video club

Su:
What films are we going to order for next term?

Mal:
It's up to us Su. The Club have made up a list we can choose from, but they are leaving it up to us to pick any 12 films from their selection, one for each week of term. We have to do the designs for the posters for the first two films.

Su:
Let's see. We always show films on Wednesday afternoons. According to my diary the first Wednesday of term falls on the 6th of January. What are we charging this time?

Mal:
Ten pence.

Su:
At that price they should come rolling in. Where are we showing the films? In the Lecture Hall?

Mal:
That's up to us. Any fair size room will do, as long as we have blackout.

Su:
Blackout?

Mal:
Yes. Do you remember last year? We designed some great posters. But the room we showed the films in was useless. The sun came streaming in and spoilt the films. We've got to get it right this time.

Su:
Yes. Come on then, let's get on with it.

TASKS

1. Working in pairs, organise your film dates for the term, assuming there is no break in the date sequence.
2. First, have a discussion with your partner and then select 12 films from the list on pages 166 and 167 to be shown on these dates. Keep in mind the kind of films your fellow students may want to see.
3. Design two attractive posters on A3 or A4 to advertise your first two films. You should use your initiative to introduce any additional information you may need.

Every which way but Loose.	Clint Eastwood and Clyde, The Orang Utan, comedy.
10.	Comedy with Dudley Moore and Bo Derek.
Superman, The Movie.	Christopher Reeve as Clark Kent alias Superman.
The Gauntlet.	Action-packed thriller starring Clint Eastwood.
The Enforcer.	Clint Eastwood as Dirty Harry, final of trilogy.
Badlands.	Star-crossed young lovers kill to stay together.
Beyond Poseidon Adventure.	Thriller about survivors on the sunken liner.
Hooper.	Burt Reynolds as the world's greatest Stuntman.
Exorcist 2—The Heretic.	Terrifying sequel to the famous shocker 'The Exorcist'.
Bugs Bunny Roadrunner Movie.	Cartoon for all starring Bugs, Daffy, Elmer and Co.
Enter the Dragon.	Stars Bruce Lee, the Martial Arts Legend.
The Exorcist.	Linda Blair as 12-year-old possessed by demons.
Dirty Harry.	Clint Eastwood as the silent cop who kills.
Magnum Force.	Sequel to Dirty Harry, prior to The Enforcer.
Blazing Saddles.	Mel Brookes comedy of how the West was not won.
The Wild Bunch.	A violent Western about men who lived brutally.
A Star is Born.	Musical romance starring Barbara Streisand.
Deliverance.	A canoe trip turns into a nightmare for 4 men.
East of Eden.	James Dean won an Oscar in the classic role.
Rod Stewart Live in LA.	Rod Stewart sings all the big hits.
Woodstock.	Famous film of the legendary concert.
Any Which Way you Can.	Clint Eastwood and Clyde return again.
Private Benjamin.	Goldie Hawn joins the Army with hilarious results.
All the President's Men.	Newspaper reporters untangle the trail to Watergate.
The Outlaw Josey Wales.	Violent Western with Clint Eastwood at his best.
Death Sport.	A glimpse of a violent future society where Death rules.
Friday the 13th.	Ultimate horror film set in closed summer camp.

Mad Max.	Horror film set in a future unruly society.
Oh God.	Outrageous comedy with George Burns as God.
Freebie and the Bean.	Comedy with two cops causing unbelievable chaos.
The Damned.	War film set in Germany when time is running out.
Death in Venice.	Dirk Bogarde in a film set in plague-ridden Venice.
Superman 2.	Continuing saga of Superman versus evil forces.
Sphinx.	Egyptian thriller starring Lesley Ann Down.
Meteor.	A comet causes disaster, starring Sean Connery, sci fi.
Bobby Deerfield.	The eternal emotional triangle, with Al Pacino.
Uptown Saturday Night.	Story of gangland feuding starring Sidney Poitier.
Oh God, Book 2.	Follow up to Oh God, John Denver and George Burns.
Jeremiah Johnson.	Violent mid-19th century saga, stars Robert Redford.
When Time Ran Out.	Disaster movie as a volcano erupts, Paul Newman.
Straight Time.	An ex-con breaks parole, starring Dustin Hoffman.
Bonnie and Clyde.	Film of the famous gangster duo, Warren Beatty.
The Green Berets.	All-action war film with the one and only John Wayne.
Hang 'em High.	Clint Eastwood survives a lynching & seeks revenge.
Bananas.	A Woody Allen romantic comedy set in deep south.
Rocky.	Award winning boxing film stars Sylvester Stallone.
Casablanca.	Winner of 3 Oscars, one of the Screen greats.
French Connection 2.	Excellent sequel to the original 'French Connection'
Chariots of Fire.	Superb award winning film of 1924 Olympics.
The Fury.	Horror film about the direction of people's minds.
9–5.	Hilarious comedy with Jane Fonda and Dolly Parton.
History of World Part 1.	Mel Brookes view of the evolution of modern man.
Kagemusha.	Film of the year, about 16th century warriors.
The Janitor.	John Hurt as the Janitor witnesses a murder.
Star Wars.	Box office sci-fi spectacular for all the family.

Searchin' for you

Rebel Sound are going to cut a new single called 'Searchin' for You' and they are looking for an original design for the record sleeve. The lyrics are included to give you the right atmosphere when you are ready to develop your ideas on paper. Your final design should reflect a recognisable scene from the lyrics.

Musical note: This is a rocker with plenty of sax and other brass instruments mixed with driving blues guitar.

I take in a movie for some light relief
I could give in but I can't be beat
I'll spend my days and nights
Searchin' for you in the streets

Make my mind up to head on home
Sick and tired of spending time alone
My two dogs just look like plates of meat
Worn out searchin' for you in the streets

Can't avoid the teacher who comes up to me
'Remember Mr Grey who taught you history?'
I say 'Who needs to know about all those historical feats?'
'I got my geography to help me search for you in the streets'

I gotta meet and tell you the news
People don't like being abused
You're such a drag and full of sly conceit
I hope you're wet and cold out in the streets

Hope you grow old out in the streets
Sad and lonely out in the streets
Your're such a phoney out in the streets

Searchin' for you in the streets
Searchin' for you in the streets
Searchin' for you in the streets

(*fade*)

TASK

Design a singles record sleeve on a 7-inch square to include only the words: 'Searchin' for You.' (If you are in a band you might like to put these lyrics to music.)

Poster design

TASK

Produce a design for a poster advertising a disco in your school or college.

TASK

Using a maximum of 6 words and any suitable illustration, design a poster on A4 on *one* of the following topics:

- Improving safety at work
- Encouraging the general public to give blood
- Health care or advice for the elderly
- Reducing cigarette consumption
- Improving safety in the home
- Encouraging physical health
- Recruiting kidney donors

'Cartoon time'

TASK

These cartoons are to be printed in a popular daily newspaper. Think of amusing punchlines.

13 Tables, charts and graphs

170 We may find that the most effective way of communicating certain types of information is by constructing graphs or charts or tables. Here is a description of top selling records presented in a way which is difficult to grasp at first reading. How could this information be better presented?

> The top selling record for the week ending thirtieth of November 1979 is 'See You' which has sold three hundred and seventy three thousand copies. The second best selling single is 'Angel Delight' which has sold two hundred and fourteen thousand copies, followed in third place by 'Dancin' Tune' which sold one hundred and ninety four thousand copies. In fourth place is 'Longshot' which has sold one hundred and eighty thousand copies and in fifth place 'Invaders' with sales topping one hundred and thirty four thousand copies.

Tables

Although this description is accurate, it is tedious to read and is therefore an example of ineffective communication. If we want to present the top selling singles for a particular week, it would be much easier to present our information in the form of a table:

Singles record chart for 30 November 1979

Title track	*Copies sold*
Angel Delight	214 000
Lost and Found	83 000
Dancin' Tune	194 000
Marvellous Weather	96 500
Say Hello to Me	27 000
See You	373 000
Long Shot	180 000
Invaders	134 000
Stetson Shuffle	97 000
Searchin' for You	43 000

While this is an improvement we are still not presenting the information in the most effective way. It is not easy to know what the third best selling record is, or how 'high' our favourite record is in the charts. This is a more satisfactory way of arranging the table:

Singles record chart for 30 November 1979

Position	*Title of record*	*No of copies sold*
1	See You	373 000
2	Angel Delight	214 000
3	Dancin' Tune	194 000
4	Long Shot	180 000
5	Invaders	134 000
6	Stetson Shuffle	97 000
7	Marvellous Weather	96 500
8	Lost and Found	83 000
9	Searchin' for You	43 000
10	Say Hello to Me	27 000

When the information is presented in this way it is easy to read and gives an instant and accurate picture of record sales for one particular week. We can also gather other useful information from the table. The use of the 'Position' column on the left-hand side of the table not only places our favourite record in the top 10 accurately, but it introduces a 'ranking' order that shows us clearly the *relative* importance of each position. For example, although 'Marvellous Weather' occupies 7th position, it is only a tiny 500 copies behind 'Stetson Shuffle' which is a huge 37 000 copies behind 'Invaders'.

Exercise

The following table shows the number of people in UK prisons. Reorganise and rewrite the table in any way you wish to improve the quality of the presentation:

Average daily population in UK prisons

Women	*Year*	*Men*
1700	1979	48 000
1700	1980	47 900
1200	1971	44 900
1100	1961	31 500
1600	1978	48 000
1500	1976	47 500
1100	1966	36 400

Reading tables

One important point to keep in mind when we look at tables is that we should first establish what the figures and letters are referring to. Look at the table on page 172 and think of questions you might want to ask before you can work out what the table is communicating.

Young Workers' League

		Home					Away					
	P	W	D	L	F	A	W	D	L	F	A	Pts
Albion	10	4	1	0	9	2	2	2	1	6	4	21
Town Rovers	10	3	1	1	14	5	3	0	2	7	7	19
Athletic	10	3	2	0	14	6	2	1	2	6	4	18
Swans	10	4	0	1	12	4	2	0	3	6	8	18
Rangers	10	4	1	0	17	3	1	1	3	5	8	17
Parkside	10	3	1	1	17	5	2	1	2	4	6	17
Dovedale	10	3	1	1	13	9	2	0	3	7	6	16
Dynamo	10	3	1	1	7	5	2	0	3	6	9	16

If you know nothing about football league tables, the above information would simply be a collection of meaningless letters and numbers. But once you have the 'key' to what the letters mean the table makes a lot of sense. Reading from left to right each letter at the top of the table means:

P = Total number of matches played at home and away
So Albion have played 10 matches
W = Games won at home
Albion have won 4 games at home
D = Games drawn at home
Albion have drawn 1 game at home
L = Games lost at home
Albion haven't lost a game at home
F = The number of goals Albion have scored at home
A = The number of goals scored against Albion at home
W = Games won away from home on the opponent's ground
D = Games drawn away from home
L = Games lost away from home
F = Goals scored away from home
A = Goals conceded away from home
Pts = The number of points each team has got
Albion are at the top of the league table with 21 points

Exercise

1 Which team has won the most games away from home?
2 Which team(s) has scored the most goals away from home?
3 Which team(s) has scored most goals at home?

Often we are confused by information contained in tables, not because the information is difficult to understand but because we do not carefully read the table to find out what each part of the table is telling us. Once we have cracked the code, tables can be interesting and informative. We can also make decisions on the basis of information contained in tables. For example, supposing you wanted to take a friend to see any one of the following games in the Young Workers' League:

- Albion versus Town Rovers
- Dovedale versus Dynamo
- Rangers versus Swans.

By looking at the table you might decide that the match between Albion and Town Rovers would be the best game as both teams are highly placed in the table.

Pictograms

Pictograms are very simple pictures or signs which convey information to the observer. The most common pictograms are the symbols used in road traffic signs, such as 'Keep left' or 'Mini-roundabout'.

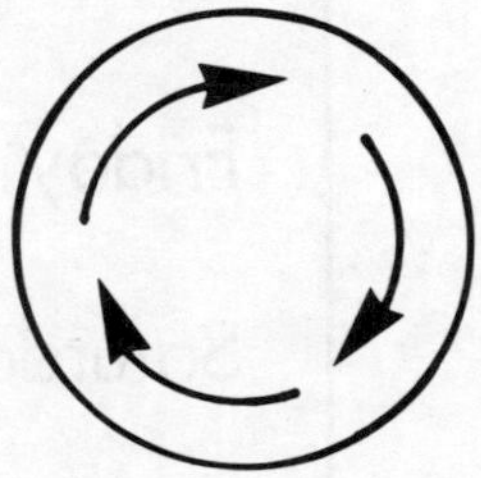

These pictures are so common in our society that we take them for granted and it is difficult to imagine a time when they did not exist. This is because shapes and colours are easily embedded in our thinking when we are constantly exposed to them. They help us to make decisions immediately, almost without thinking. Thus a car driver responds automatically to a traffic sign and a non-smoker seeks that tell-tale non-smoking symbol on the side of a railway carriage.

Yet though we react quickly to signs and symbols they remain symbols only and do not really become part of our thinking process. Everybody knows what a British Rail sign is when they see one, but how many of us can actually draw this extremely simple shape from memory?

Exercise

Without reference to any documents

- Describe the sequence of traffic lights.
- Describe a 'No Overtaking' traffic sign.
- Describe the scene depicted in the BBC colour test card.

To the communicator, pictograms can be useful in presenting basic information in a more attractive package. This pictogram shows the number of hours young people spend watching TV.

TV viewing—young people

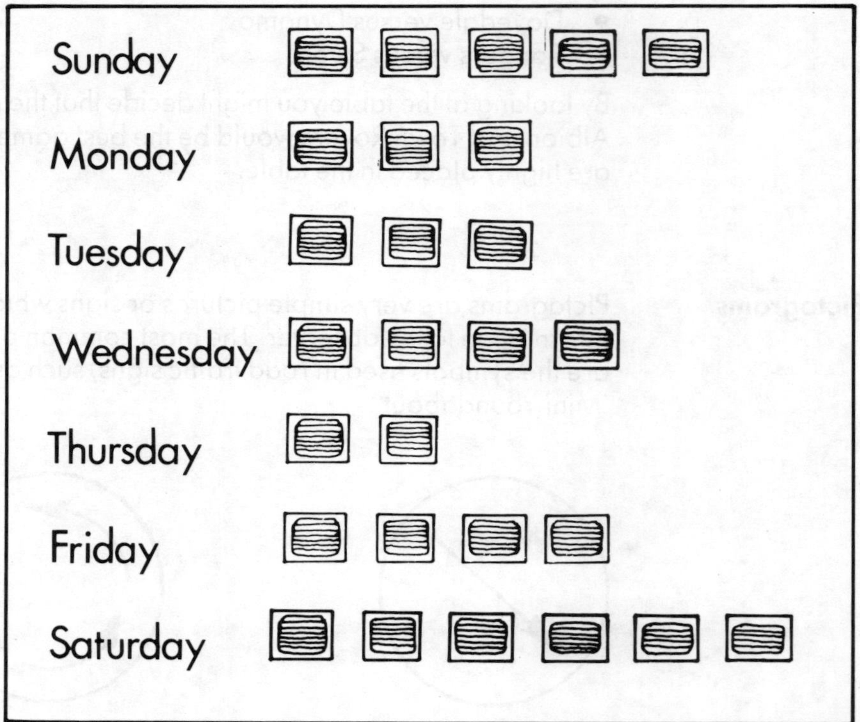

Each ▤ represents one hour's viewing

- Which day do young people watch the most TV?
- Which day do young people watch the least TV?
- How much TV on average does a young person watch in a week?

When you come to draw a pictogram it is always helpful if you can make your drawings look like the actual subject matter you are describing. In the previous pictogram each little drawing represents one hour's viewing.

Exercise Look at the following table and present the information in the form of a pictogram:

Number of hours spent playing records

Day	*Sun*	*Mon*	*Tues*	*Wed*	*Thurs*	*Fri*	*Sat*
No of hours playing records	3	1	1	2	3	2	4

Pie charts

Another method of presenting information is by using pie charts. A circle or 'pie' is drawn and then divided into parts or slices, each slice usually representing a percentage of the total.

If we wanted to make known the sales of Plastic Records Ltd as:

- 50 per cent record albums and 45s
- 25 per cent posters
- 25 per cent hi-fi equipment

it would be much simpler to present the information as:

Total sales

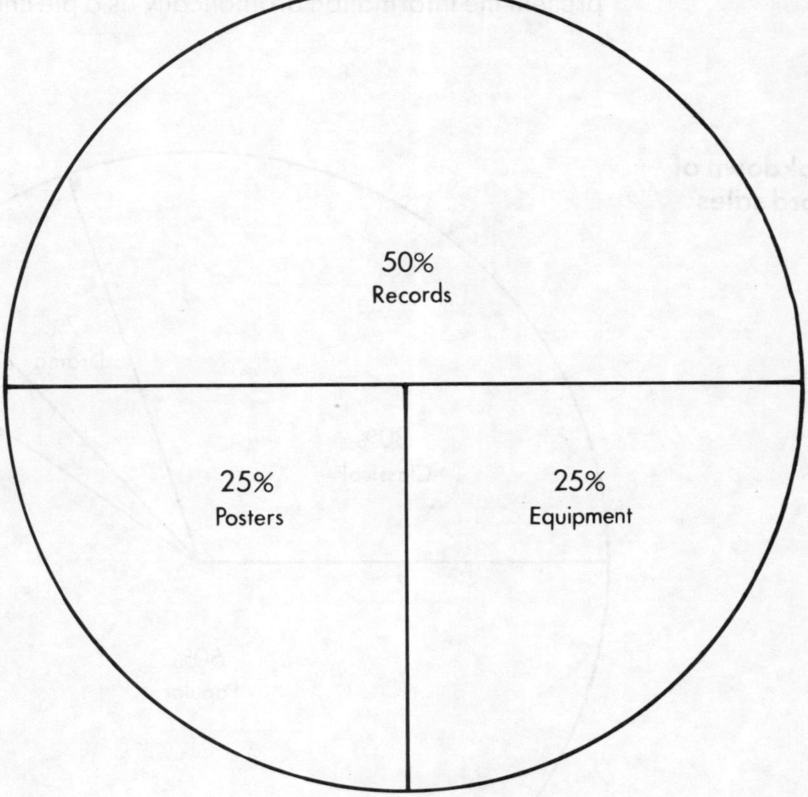

The chart shows the turnover of stock in percentage terms clearly and precisely. The three slices of the pie represent the 3 types of sale.

We can use a pie chart to show more detailed information. For example, we know that 50 per cent of sales are records, but we don't know what kind of records are being sold. When we come to look at the company's files we find that record sales are broken down as:

- Popular: 60 per cent
- Classical: 30 per cent
- Drama: 7 per cent
- Poetry: 3 per cent

In order to transfer these percentages accurately to a pie chart we have to multiply each percentage by 3.6. This gives us the correct number of degrees to count off on our circle using a protractor. So

- 60 per cent multiplied by 3.6 = 216 degrees
- 30 per cent multiplied by 3.6 = 108 degrees
- 7 per cent multiplied by 3.6 = 25 degrees
- 3 per cent multiplied by 3.6 = 11 degrees

To check that these figures are correct we should be able to add them up to a total of 360 degrees.

Using a protractor to mark off the degrees on a circle we can present the information dramatically as a pie chart:

Breakdown of record sales

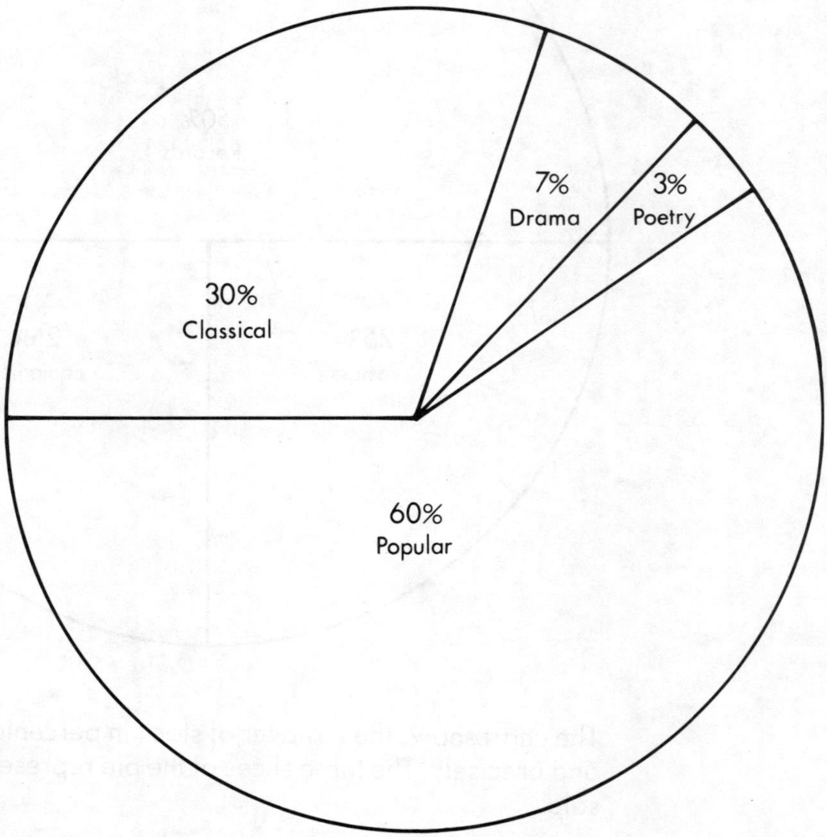

Pie charts are also used to show how some things are divided up. We can use different patterns or colours to separate the big divisions. The chart on page 177 shows the facilities used at a Leisure Centre during one month. Each slice represents the facility being used on 10 occasions.

Use of leisure centre

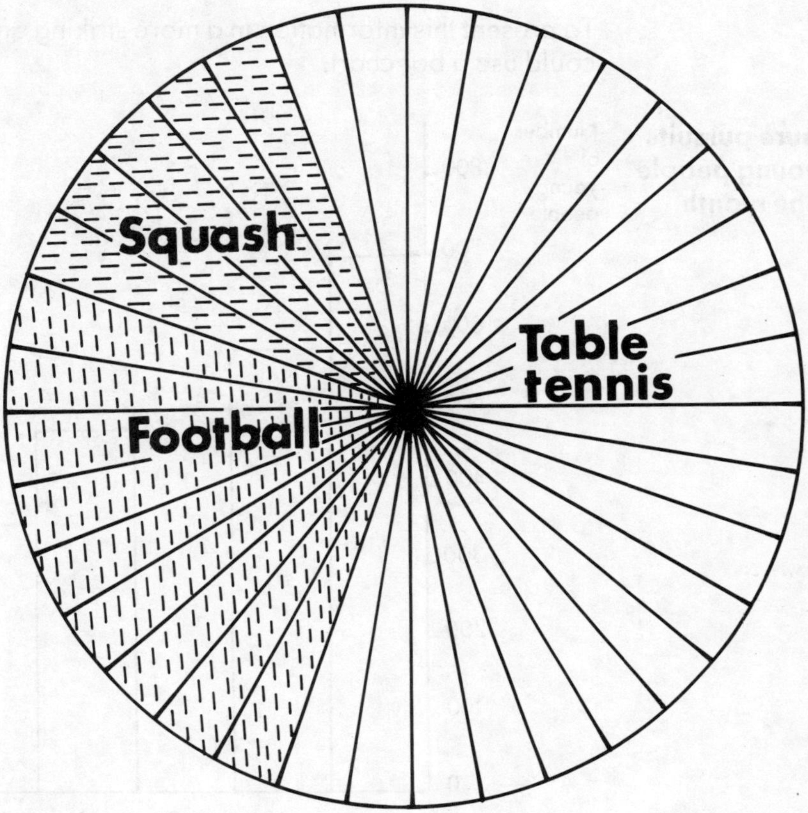

- How many times was squash played?
- How many times did people play table tennis?
- What is the total number of individual games played in one month?

Exercise In Britain, the total energy consumed is in the following proportions: electricity 5 per cent, gas 21 per cent, petroleum 36 per cent, coal 38 per cent. Produce a pie chart showing these proportions.

Bar charts

Bar charts are easy to construct and easy to understand. They provide an effective way of showing more complicated information that cannot be presented as a pie chart.

A recent survey on the leisure activities of 1000 young people in a northern town found that 700 young people went to the cinema once a month, 580 went to three local youth clubs, 500 went to a disco, 490 attended football matches, and 350 went to a rock concert.

To present this information in a more striking and dramatic way we could use a bar chart:

Leisure pursuits of young people in one month

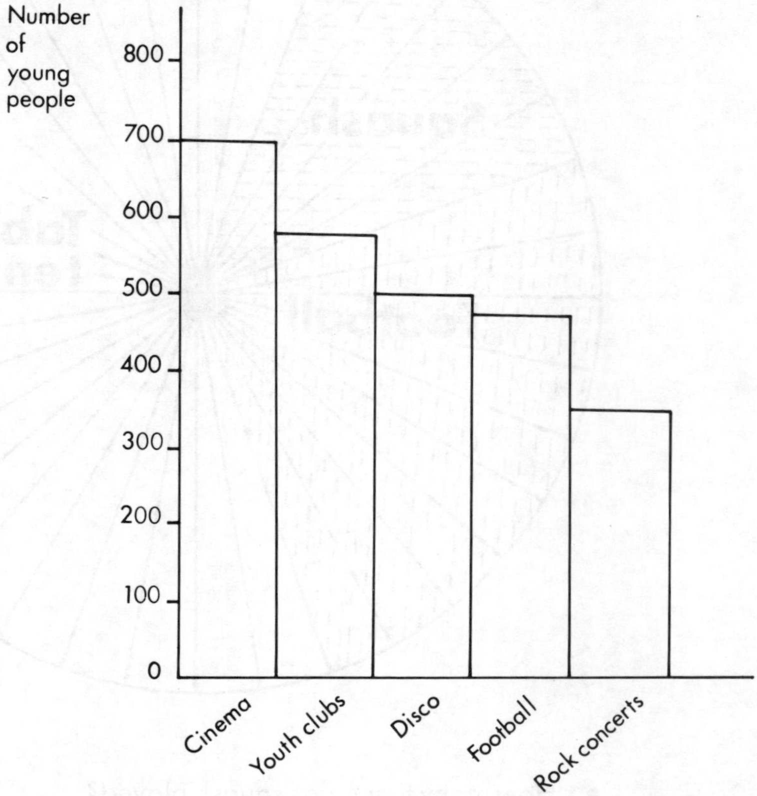

You can see that the information has been plotted along two lines, a vertical line and a horizontal line. The bars on a bar chart can be either upright or horizontal. The most important thing to keep in mind is that the information should be clearly labelled so the reader is in no doubt about what the figures and shapes mean.

Exercise

Construct a similar bar chart for leisure activities of young people which was carried out in 1961 in the same town. One thousand young people were interviewed and the survey showed that 950 visited the cinema, 780 went ten-pin bowling, 600 went to football matches, 500 went roller skating and 250 went to their local dance hall.

When you have completed the bar chart, compare your findings with those in the recent survey. Make a note of the differences between the two charts.

Interpreting the information

You will notice that the cinema was far more popular then than it is now, that there were no discos, and that young people went ten-pin bowling. Ten-pin bowling was a sport which was very popular in the late 1950s and 1960s. This leads us to ask certain questions about information presented in these charts. For example, why was the cinema so popular? Why didn't young people visit youth clubs?

Exercise

Write down why you think the cinema was more popular in 1961 than it is today.

Seeing behind the information

What you are trying to do is to offer an explanation and to give some thought about the information presented in the two charts. Bar charts, like tables and graphs, are just another way of passing on information. They are essentially telling us something, and as with all information we receive we have to ask ourselves serious questions.

By using our intelligence and imagination we can work out that in 1961 young people had much less entertainment than they have now and there were fewer films on TV, which in any case were all shown in black-and-white on only two channels!

Exercise

Look at the double bar chart below and answer these questions:

1 Why have motoring offences increased during the summer months?
2 Why have burglaries decreased in the autumn?
3 Why have motoring and burglary offences increased during December?

Serious motoring and burglary offences recorded at a police station from July to December

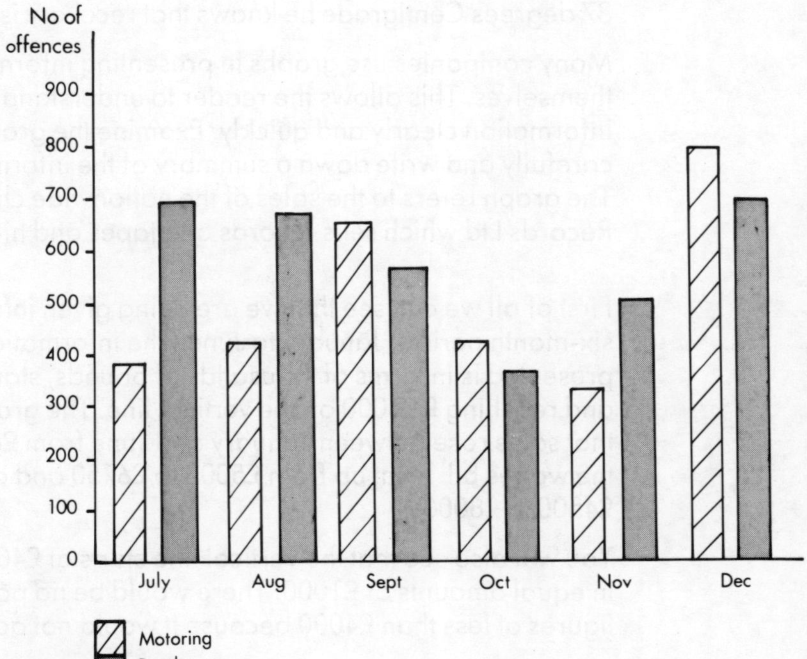

Looking at the bar chart on page 179 we notice that December has the highest number of recorded motoring offences. We know that late December is Christmas-time with parties and evenings out and maybe the reason for the high number of serious motoring offences such as drinking and driving.

We can also see that burglaries are more numerous in July and August. We know that this is the time of the year when people often take their annual holiday and that their houses are left empty. We note also that the number of burglaries is high during December.

Again, during this time of the year people will have presents lying about the house and these will provide rich pickings for the burglar.

Although it is important that a bar chart is neat and accurate, it is much more important for us to understand its real meaning thoroughly.

Graphs

We can take certain types of information and present them as a graph on ordinary graph paper. A graph is often the most satisfactory way of showing how things vary. For example, hospital patients' temperatures are always plotted on graph paper, with their temperatures recorded against the vertical line and the time period along the bottom line. In other words, the bottom line is best used for fixed things such as hours, days, months and years and the upright or vertical line for what varies such as temperatures, wage levels and prices. When our hospital doctor can see that our daily temperature is levelling out at about 37 degrees Centigrade he knows that recovery is on the way.

Many companies use graphs in presenting information about themselves. This allows the reader to understand a lot of information clearly and quickly. Examine the graph on page 181 carefully and write down a summary of the information it contains. The graph refers to the sales of the nationwide chain Plastic Records Ltd which sells records and tapes and hi-fi equipment.

First of all we can see that we are being given information for a six-month period, January to June. The information being presented is in terms of thousands of pounds, starting with £4000 and reaching £12 000 on the vertical line. The graph also tells us that sales rose between January and June from £8000 to £11 000, the wages bill went up from £5000 to £6750 and costs rose from £4500 to £8000.

You will also see that the vertical line starts at £4000 and advances in equal amounts of £1000. There would be no point in starting the figures at less than £4000 because it would not add to our

Plastic Records Ltd half-year statistics

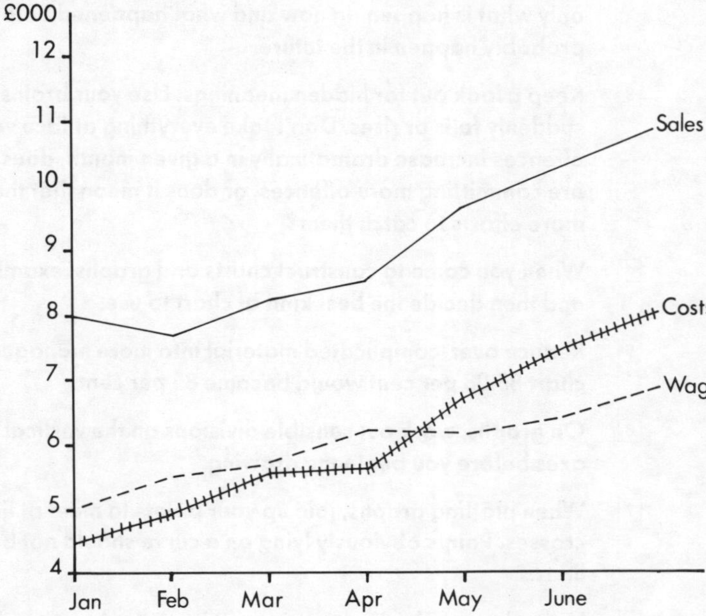

knowledge. Equally, we round off our figures to the nearest thousand because these are convenient divisions for our particular needs.

Exercise

Plastic Records Ltd achieved the following sales between July and December. Construct a graph to include this information:

Month	*Records*	*Cassettes*	*Posters*	*T-shirts*
July	*5 000*	*4 500*	*6 000*	*7 500*
August	*5 800*	*5 000*	*7 500*	*8 000*
September	*6 500*	*6 000*	*8 000*	*8 500*
October	*4 500*	*7 500*	*8 500*	*9 500*
November	*7 500*	*7 580*	*9 000*	*10 500*
December	*10 500*	*9 500*	*11 500*	*12 000*

Sales in £000s for records, cassettes, posters and T-shirts.

The advantages of presenting information in tables or charts or graphs is that we can get our points over quickly and we make life easier for the reader. Also, as you will have noted, the visual presentation of information has an impact which is important in terms of communicating ideas and trends.

Tips on graphs and charts

1. Always take your time looking at graphs and charts. Make sure you understand all the signs and symbols.

2. Pay particular attention to trends. Charts are basically pictures that tell us not only what is happening now and what happened before but what will probably happen in the future.

3. Keep a look out for hidden meanings. Use your brains to work out why a line suddenly falls or rises. Don't take everything at face value. If motoring offences increase dramatically in a given month, does this mean that drivers are committing more offences, or does it mean that the police are making more efforts to catch them?

4. When you come to construct charts and graphs, examine your material first and then decide the best kind of chart to use.

5. Reduce over-complicated material into more manageable units. So, for a pie chart 85.08 per cent would become 85 per cent.

6. On graphs, work out sensible divisions on the vertical and horizontal lines or axes before you begin the drawing.

7. When plotting graphs, join up your points to meet at lightly marked pencil crosses. Points obviously lying on a curve should not be joined by straight lines.

8. Use colour or shading to bring out important points—but don't overdo this.

Crime beat

TASK

The table on page 183 shows how successful the police were in combating crime in the UK over a 10-year period.

1. Looking at the table generally, how would you describe the overall success of the police force over the 10-year period? Is there an obvious trend to be detected? Explain.

2. What is meant by burglary?

Clear-up rates for serious offences

Percentages

	England & Wales		*Scotland*		*Northern Ireland*	
	1971	*1980*	*1971*	*1980*	*1971*	*1980*
Serious offences recorded						
• Violence against the person	82	77	87	82	28	55
• Sexual offences	76	74	68	62	87	65
• Burglary	37	31	26	22	27	20
• Robbery	42	29	29	27	7	20
• Theft and handling stolen goods	43	39	37	30	46	25
• Fraud and forgery	83	75	80	82	84	60
• Criminal damage	34	28	32	20	10	16
Total serious offences	45	40	38	33	32	26

3 If you wanted to know from this table how successful the police were in catching vandals, where would you look?

4 What was the overall clear-up rate in Scotland in 1980?

5 What are the clear-up rates for serious offences in England and Wales and Northern Ireland in 1980? Can you think of a reason why the police are less successful in Northern Ireland?

6 Look at the rates for 'Violence against the person' and 'Burglary' in any country. Can you work out why the police are more successful in one than they are in the other? (This is a difficult question.)

7 Why are the police so good at catching frauds and forgers and so bad at catching thieves? (This is a more difficult question.)

Night life

184

How we spend our evening leisure in England and Wales

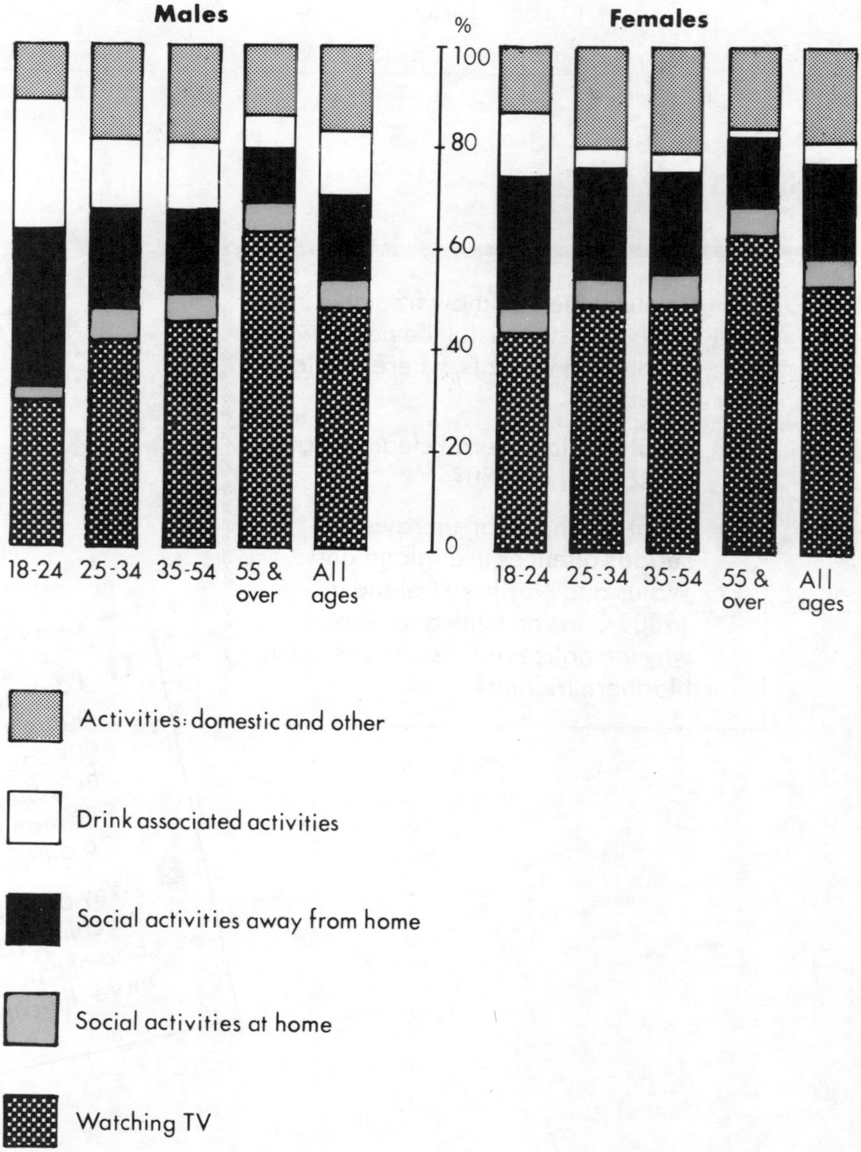

TASK

1. Looking at the chart on page 184 generally, what leisure activity would you say females liked more than males, and what do males like more than females?
2. As a general observation, in what ways do leisure activities change as men and women get older?
3. Approximately what percentage of time do women aged between 18 and 24 spend on drink-associated activities?
4. Give some examples to show that you know the meaning of the phrase 'drink-associated activities'.
5. Why do you think young men spend more time than women on drink-associated activities?
6. Young women spend approximately 42 per cent of their time watching TV, and young men 30 per cent. Write down some reasons to explain this difference.
7. Why do domestic activities tend to increase in middle life?
8. Do you think there is anything missing from this chart? Jot down what you think it is, and any other points you would like to make of a critical kind.

Down the table

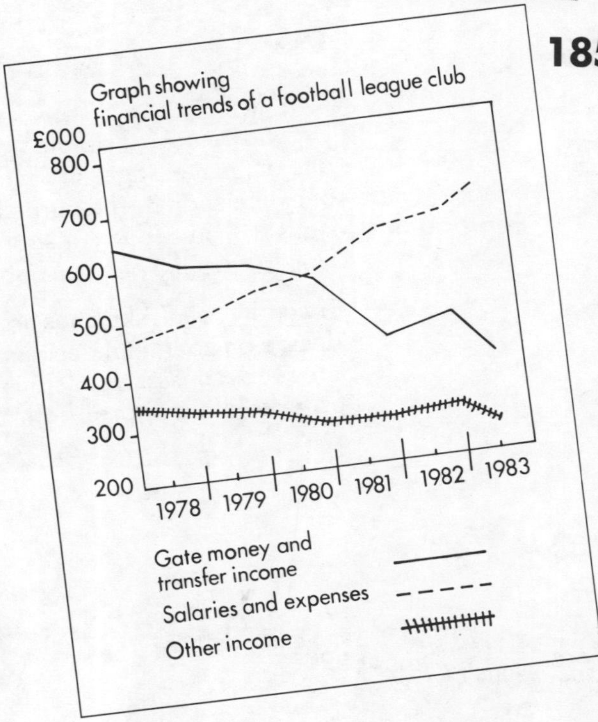

TASK

1. Approximately how much money was earned by the club during 1982?
2. Approximately how much money was spent by the club during 1982?
3. During what season would you guess the main spectator stand burned down?
4. How would you describe the financial state of the club during the 1982/83 season? Support your description with facts.
5. What is transfer income?
6. Make a list of possible sources of 'other income'.

Signs

186

TASK

Draw a picture or simple sign to convey one of the messages in Section A and one in Section B. The purpose of the signs will be either to instruct or to direct members of the general public.

Try a few rough sketches first before you decide on your final designs. When you are ready, design your signs on A4, using colour if appropriate.

Section A: Instructional signs indicating:

This is the way in
This is the way out
Stay out of here
We prefer dogs on a lead
You should wear goggles for this job
Always wear a helmet
We don't allow talking or noise in here
Sensible people wash their hands before leaving

Section B: Directional signs indicating:

Football pitch
Swimming area
Scrap yard
Disco dancing
Roller skating
Car test centre
Recording studio
Rubbish dump

Weighty matters

We want to give you some idea of your ideal weight. Not that we can tell you anything you don't know already. Some people's poundage might be anything up to 7 lb either side of the 'ideal' weight for the *medium-frame* figure. Anyhow, here's the ladies' weights first. Remember, all the weights given are without shoes but include about 3 lb for indoor clothing. (Note: 1 kilogramme = 2.2 lb.)

Women

The tall woman of 6 ft should expect to come out at about 11 stone, and the tiny woman of 5 ft about 8 stone. Since most of us are in between, here is a list:

5ft 1in = 8 stone 3 lb
5ft 2in = 8 stone 7 lb
5ft 3in = 8 stone 9 lb
5ft 4in = 8 stone 12 lb
5ft 5in = 9 stone 1 lb
5ft 6in = 9 stone 5 lb
5ft 7in = 9 stone 9 lb
5ft 8in = 9 stone 12 lb
5ft 9in = 10 stone 2 lb
5ft 10in = 10 stone 5 lb
5ft 11in = 10 stone 10 lb

Men

Now here's our chart for men. Of course, height for height we must expect men to be somewhat heavier than women because of that extra bone and muscle development:

Stones (lb)	*height*	*Stones (lb)*	*height*
13 0	6ft 3	10 9	5ft 8
12 8	6ft 2	10 5	5ft 7
12 3	6ft 1	10 1	5ft 6
11 12	6ft 0	9 10	5ft 5
11 8	5ft 11	9 7	5ft 4
11 4	5ft 10	9 4	5ft 3
10 13	5ft 9	9 1	5ft 2

TASK

Reassemble all this factual information into one table under suitable headings. Include a short introduction of important information.

Bar charts

188

TASK

Construct bar charts or any other suitable devices to convey the following information in a more interesting way:

Growth in electronic equipment in British living rooms

	1981	*1983*
Teletext TV	2%	7%
Video recorders	10%	28%
Home computers	1%	8%
Video game consoles	2%	6%

Foreign imports into Britain in 1982

	1982
Teletext TV	8%
Video recorders	100%
Home computers	60%
Video game consoles	100%

Graphs

TASK

Draw a neat graph to include the following information:

Total attendances at football league matches

Season	*England and Wales Division One*	*All Scotland*
1979–80	12 163 000	3 381 000
1980–81	11 393 000	2 871 000
1981–82	10 421 000	2 844 000

Beneath the graph, suggest reasons why there is such a decline in attendances and draw up a list of proposals that might stop or reverse the process.

TASKS FOR GROUPS

1 Count the number of 'live' teeth you have. If you have more than 32 contact the Guinness Book of Records. Set out the group's teeth count in this way:

Teeth survey

Total number in survey___ Average age of group members___

Number of teeth	*Number in group*	*%*
*Complete set of 32	—	—
29 to 31	—	—
26 to 28	—	—
23 to 25	—	—
20 to 22	—	—
17 to 19	—	—
16 or less	—	—

*Permanent teeth sometimes continue to appear up to the age of 20+.

Now present your findings in the form of a pie chart. You may like to carry out the same research on an older age group and present both results together as a bar chart.

2 Complete a similar survey on *one* of the following topics. If your group is too small you are allowed to extend the area of research outside the group.

a Weekly expenditure on alcohol
b Average daily consumption of cigarettes or tobacco
c Number of hours participating in or watching non-TV sport in one week
d Number of hours spent reading in one week *or* listening to radio
e Monthly expenditure on clothes *or* make-up *or* music
f Weekly expenditure on travel

14 Assignments

190 *Notes on assignments:* Both asssignments are designed to be completed by small groups of students working in teams. When you read the assignments through you will realise that there is plenty to do, and some of it looks difficult. This is why you are in a team. You are only expected to do a fair share of the work, and what you do and what the others do is a matter for your team to decide—so put your heads together and sort out a fair system of work sharing. Of course, this doesn't mean you will be left alone with a difficult problem. You can discuss your problems with anybody in the team and it might prevent you making silly mistakes. *Read each assignment thoroughly* **before** *you begin the tasks.*

Assignment 1

The Mayfield Sports Centre

The Mayfield Indoor Sports Centre has been open for 10 years and has been a great success with the public and the local community. To celebrate the centre's anniversary a 'Competition Day' is being planned featuring the top players and teams taking part in the centre's most popular sports: soccer six, squash and badminton.

All the following tasks lead to one final objective: that is, can your team organise and promote a 'Competition Day' for the centre? There are many decisions to be made and your team will have to make them. Before you start the tasks read the Factsheet at the end of this assignment (page 194).

TASK ONE—the letter

1

In the local newspaper you see the following advertisement:

The Sports Council of Great Britain invites local sports clubs and societies to apply for a grant of up to £150 for any approved activity which is designed to encourage organised sport in this region. The Council requests that all interested parties apply, in writing, giving brief particulars of proposals to: The Sports Council of Great Britain 70 Brompton Road, London, SW3.

Discuss in your team what you intend to include in this letter and *write it out in full as a business letter*. You must produce fairly sound arguments to convince the Sports Council of the value of having a 'Competition Day'. You will want to stress the success of the centre and point out that you hope the day's events will interest non-members and help promote the health aspects of sport in the local community.

TASK TWO—rules of the game

2

Because of the differences in interpretation of the rules of the three sports (soccer six, squash and badminton singles), it is necessary to *draw up some basic rules for all three games* so that all the players and spectators are fully informed in advance. You will probably have to do some research on this and to negotiate in your group to arrive at a consensus. If there is real disagreement you may have to take a vote. The most important differences in rules will probably apply to soccer six.

3

TASK THREE—advertising

Of course no 'Competition Day' can be successful without the right kind of publicity. You must therefore make a decision about this. You have been allowed about £50 and you can spend this on poster advertising or/and a 3-minute advertising slot on local commercial radio.

When you have made up your mind about this you will produce:

a *A neat poster design*, in two colours, which must convey all the basic information about the competition (read about posters in Chapter 12 first). Then, on a separate sheet of paper, write the name and telephone number of a suitable printer from the *Yellow Pages*.

or/and

b *Produce a lively and convincing 3-minute script* to promote the competition on local radio. This must then be recorded on tape for the guidance of the programme producer at the local radio station. An alternative to this would be to *produce a similar product on video* to be shown in the local schools, clubs and sports centres.

4

TASK FOUR—planning the fixtures

Now you will have to get down to the nitty-gritty of *planning the match fixtures*. You can decide either to have a knock-out competition or you can organise each round of sporting activity on a league basis (or a combined league and knock-out). This is up to you. Remember you want to get through a lot of events during the afternoon. The 'Competition Day' will start at 2.30 pm and finish at 6 pm. The players and teams opposite are listed in their current league positions and represent the two top divisions in each sport:

4

Soccer six		Squash (Women)
League One	*League Two*	*League position*
Hadden Colts	Dark Blues	Beresford
Moorehouse	Ashton	Lindley
Charter X	Keaton Rovers	Frances
Rangers	Sporting Aces	Winstanley
All Stars	Downtown	Mansell
Brasshouse	Wildon	Draper
Temple Tigers	Proteus	Porter
Beacon	Sandon	Armfield

Badminton (Men)		Squash (Men)	
League One	*League Two*	*League One*	*League Two*
Hands	Houssain	Amery	Singh
Kettle	Singh	Clifford	Hazel
Khan	Hutchings	Watt	Facy
Coker	Davies	Grainger	Wharton
Richards	Kennedy	Butt	Barry
Harris	Meade	Banja	Mercer
Patel	Jackson		
McFarland	Worrell		

When planning the fixtures you want to make sure that:

a there is enough time between each game for rest periods

b a 45-minute interval is allowed for spectators and players to get refreshments

c the final of each competition is to take place at different times to allow spectators to see the best of all the action

d a short period of time is allowed for at the end of the games for the presentation of trophies and medals.

You should remember that when deciding the order of play it is best in the opening stages of the competition to arrange for teams or players of similar ability to play each other. For example, with soccer six you wouldn't start with Hadden Colts playing Sandon. On paper, Hadden should win and probably would, but if they were drawn together in later rounds anything could happen. As in all sports, players tend to raise their game the more they progress in competitions. As an organiser, you want to ensure as much excitement and surprise as you can.

Factsheet

Sports catered for: indoor soccer, cricket, basketball, squash, weight-lifting and training, netball, judo and martial arts, badminton, self-defence, billiards and snooker, and many minority sports.

There are plans in the pipeline to establish a Basketball League and some of the profits from the 'Competition Day' will go towards buying kit and equipment.

Full membership numbers: 2986. Membership: £5 per annum. Day guests and spectators: £1.

Two resident staff and many experts are available to give private tuition by arrangement.

Open all the year round except usual Bank Holidays. The centre's facilities can be booked Monday to Saturday 9 am–6 pm. Late evenings Tuesdays and Thursdays till 11 pm.

Facilities available: substantial multiple-use indoor playing area; changing rooms with showers (men and women); 3 squash and 2 badminton courts; the 'Kung Fu' room; billiards, snooker, pool and indoor games room; reception area with soft drinks service; and elevated viewing platforms for spectators (see diagram).

Tournaments and leagues are organised through the centre on a regular basis. Coach and travelling arrangements bookable in the reception office.

Future plans. Work has already started on the construction of an all-weather floodlit full-size football pitch adjoining the centre. We hope to incorporate a treble running track for the benefit of local athletes.

Diagram of Mayfield Sports Centre

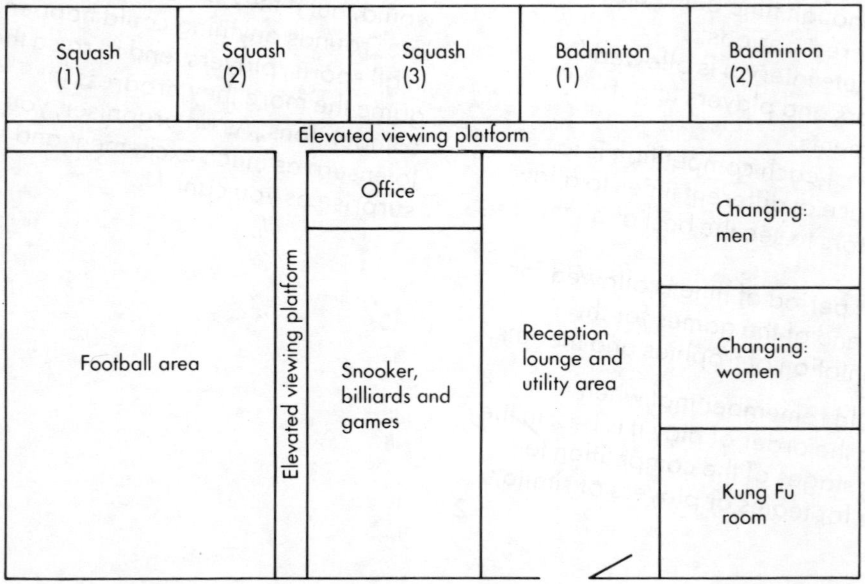

5

TASK FIVE—circular letter and map

As there are about 30 club secretaries and VIPs you would like to invite to the 'Competition Day', it is now time to send them information in the form of a *circular letter and map*. The purpose of the letter is to invite them to the competition and to provide a brief description of the day's events. (A circular letter is an identical letter sent to everybody.)

You must attach to the letter a neatly drawn street map of the area showing the position of the sports centre and clear instructions about train, bus and car-parking facilities. You will also want to design a small form which the secretary or the VIP can return to let you know whether or not they will attend the competition. (Use your imagination for this task and get hold of a street atlas to help you with the map.)

6

TASK SIX—the programme

For the day of the competition you are to *produce a two-page programme* which will be distributed free to all participants and spectators. The cost of this will be met by a local businessman, and as part of the deal you will place an advertisement in the programme for his shop. He has left the design and some of the wording to you, but you must include these words:

> Tommy Kay's Sports Shop (200 yards from the Mayfield Sports Centre). The Monday after the 'Competition Day' we will knock 15 per cent off all goods bought if the customer is carrying a Mayfield Programme.

In your programme you will include:

a a welcoming article for people at the centre. The article should say something interesting about the centre and encourage more people to join as active members.

b a list of early fixtures. (You should allow space for spectators to fill in details of teams/players involved in the later rounds.)

When your team has finished this assignment you should have produced:

- A business letter for the Sports Council.
- A set of rules for three sports.
- A poster design and/or a 3-minute scripted tape or video recording.
- A plan for the fixtures.
- A circular letter and map.
- The programme.

Assignment 2

The town plan

You live in a town called Hatton. For some years now the local newspaper, the *Hatton Herald*, has been informing its readers about the latest developments regarding the redevelopment of the town. This week's article (page 197) is particularly interesting.

TASK

You are now ready to start the tasks. The *Herald* is providing you with a rough map of the present town and a series of extracts from various reports written by experts. You must read and understand all these documents before you begin working on the tasks. Remember, you cannot please all the people all of the time. Someone somewhere is going to be disappointed.

A shot in the arm for Hatton

For many years – far more than this editor cares to remember – this paper has been campaigning for new developments in the town, especially for the provision of new housing and industry. We have consistently warned of the risks of a shrinking population and the prospects of living in a slowly dying town. At last something is beginning to stir. In last week's paper we exclusively announced the County Council's plans for redevelopment. Since then we have been flooded with mail from our readers about the Council's proposals.

What is clear is that the people of Hatton are deeply interested in what happens to their town. Mr Willis writing from Leighton Way sums up this feeling when he writes: 'Three cheers for the County Council's proposals. But a word of caution. The people of Hatton should have their say. We will have to live in the area long after the planners have gone.'

Mrs Shelley from Ashton Road up on the Carlton Estate also welcomes the news: 'The nearest hospital is 15 miles away, and this makes the journey for elderly out-patients a nightmare. Let's have the long-awaited (and promised) Hatton Cottage Hospital.'

Miss Pat Anderson who runs the Post Office on the High Street tells us: 'I'm glad to see that there are plans to build 12 small factories. We want to attract industry to Hatton to provide work and prosperity for all our citizens.'

The young have also made their voice heard. Miss Karen Birch from Fullway Road telephoned our office and said: 'Maybe the plans could include the building of a concert hall. Last week the Hatton branch of the *Rebel Sound* Fan Club had to travel 20 miles to see *Sound* in concert. This costs a lot of money and it would be great if the big bands could come to Hatton.'

What is clear is that the people of Hatton want their say, and the *Herald* will, as always, provide you with that opportunity. The *Herald* isn't a people's paper for nothing!

What we would like our readers to do is to send us their own plans and ideas about redevelopment. We will then pass on your ideas to the County Council and the *Herald* will campaign throughout the planning discussions to ensure that your voice is heard in the right quarters.

Here we outline the proposals to develop Hatton and we provide a map of the area to help you. Using this material we invite you to submit your ideas and plans. In 10 years' time we don't want to have letters from 'moaners' and 'old codgers' telling us that the people of Hatton were overlooked. Planning is about people and people should be consulted about planning. So you should now have got the message. Put on your thinking caps, get out your pens and pencils, and let's plan for the future together.

The proposals

The proposals made by the County Council are to develop vacant land and to provide both housing and employment for the coming overspill population of a nearby town. The population of Hatton is about 1500, and it is planned to provide facilities and housing for another 1000 people. The Council is aware that Hatton has some ancient historical sites and has attracted an ever growing number of visitors over the years. These sites should not be seriously disturbed by any new development.

In total, the Council wants to provide sites for:

- a school for both junior and secondary pupils
- housing for 250 families (two-thirds more houses required)
- an industrial estate consisting of premises to be used by 12 factory units
- a leisure and boating centre
- premises for five shops or a supermarket to be located on or near the new housing estate
- a bus station
- a small cottage hospital
- one other building or facility of your choice

How to complete the tasks

1. Trace all the existing features of the area on to a sheet of A4 and think carefully about where you intend to site the new additions. Draw in the additions using symbols to indicate your choice of site.

2. Joining a small group, discuss your ideas and plans, and between you, on a large piece of card, produce a plan of the new town that most fairly represents the overall opinion of your group. You should produce a colour key on a separate sheet of paper.

   When drawing the full-size plan try to keep to a reasonable scale. You must also draw in a road network to serve the new housing areas. It will be necessary to invent names for the new main roads.

3. Using an appropriate symbol and colour for bus stops, work out a sensible bus route to serve the town's population. You may draw in extra roads or modify existing roads, but all buildings must remain intact.

4. When the map is completed explain in writing the reasons for the siting of:

   - the new housing
   - the school
   - the factory units

REPORTS

The *Hatton Herald* has on behalf of our readers asked a number of experts to carry out surveys of the area of the town in order to highlight the problems involved in the proposed development plans. What follows are extracts from these reports and readers should take note of the points before submitting their plans.

Report one: Geological findings:

The main geological problems are to be found in the old mining area north of the town. The mines have been 'dead' for a quarter of a century and in the last 10 years the mine shafts have been used as 'land fill' sites...... The Clayford Industrial Waste Disposal Company has been placing industrial waste into the shafts....... This raises certain questions about the risks involved in building residential property in the area.

Report two: Conservation findings:

There are many features of the Hatton landscape which have attracted increasing numbers of tourists over the years. This in turn has provided extra trade and income for many local businesses...... Hatton Castle standing within ancient burial grounds is an essential part of local history and any threat to its existence would lead to much protest ... not just from locals... but from people and organisations concerned with national historical monuments.

Report three: Recreation:

In the last five years many residents have spent much of their own time converting the disused railway track into a 'natural pathway', providing an excellent opportunity for walkers, joggers and, more recently, the Hatton Cycle Club. No doubt the proposals for redevelopment will take into account the value of this pathway..... The river, too, is a wonderful asset to the town .... adjacent buildings of any kind would be unthinkable.

Report four: Hatton Traders Association

Trade is already suffering severely from the opening of a supermarket in Harpenden (3 miles to the east)..... Hatton does not need further retail outlets.... Shops should not be built near existing retail outlets.... This Association is prepared to negotiate for its members for the construction of trading outlets in the vicinity of Hatton Castle.

Report five: The Hatton Wildlife Group:

The stretch of river by the marsh area should not be disturbed by development...... Along these lower reaches we have noted the breeding of the Marsh Warbler...... any disturbance would threaten a valuable species...... We would like to see a wildlife sanctuary set up in this whole area of the river...... The marsh area is gaining a regional reputation as a most important nesting site for many unusual bird species.

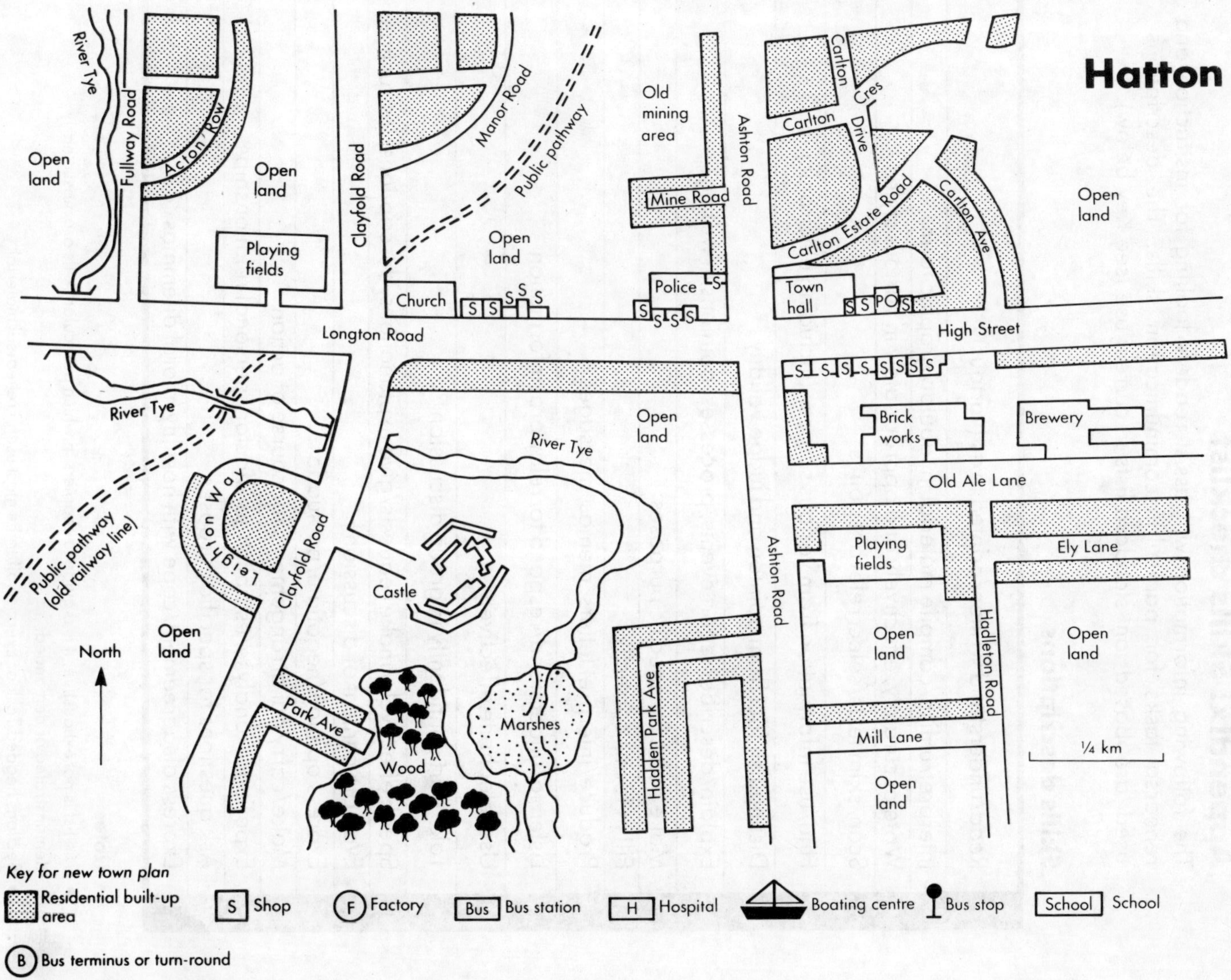
Hatton
Open land
River Tye
Fullway Road
Acton Row
Open land
Playing fields
Clayfold Road
Manor Road
Public pathway
Open land
Church
S S S S S
Old mining area
Mine Road
Ashton Road
Police
S S S S S
Carlton
Carlton Cres
Carlton Drive
Carlton Estate Road
Carlton Ave
Town hall
S S PO S
Open land
Longton Road
High Street
S S S S S S S S
Brick works
Brewery
River Tye
Open land
Old Ale Lane
Public pathway (old railway line)
Leighton Way
Clayfold Road
Castle
Playing fields
Ely Lane
Open land
North
Park Ave
Wood
Marshes
Hadden Park Ave
Ashton Road
Open land
Hadleton Road
Open land
Mill Lane
Open land
¼ km
Key for new town plan
Residential built-up area
S Shop
F Factory
Bus Bus station
H Hospital
Boating centre
Bus stop
School School
B Bus terminus or turn-round

Appendix: Skills checklist

The following information will assist readers looking for instruction and rehearsal tasks for particular communication skills. The descriptions used are based on standard lists in current use (see Key below).

Skills descriptions

Skills descriptions
Read/understand written/printed texts (various)
Interpret/utilise/compile material in tabular/graphic form
Write accurately, effectively and appropriately in various styles
Scan/skim texts/select relevant points
Find/use information from various sources (including electronic)
Distinguish fact from opinion and judge validity
Explain/describe/report events, processes, opinions in writing
Make notes for specific purposes
Fill in forms correctly
Produce/interpret letters, memos, messages
Listen to/understand/respond to/relay oral information
Use telephone effectively
Take part confidently in group discussion
Speak effectively/make requests/give explanations, descriptions, instructions
Evaluate content of discussion
Express opinion/negotiate/persuade
Make/carry out arrangements for course of action
Experience/analyse/establish satisfactory personal relationships
Ask questions for specific purposes
Express disagreement/cope with hostility/moral dilemmas

Notes

- The list is not exhaustive; it is a guide to chapters in which particular skills are most clearly demonstrated or demanded.
- Sections headed Task or Exercise offer the most useful rehearsal material.

Codes in booklets ABC	RSA	C&G	Chapters in text
6.3.1, 6.3.2 6.1, 6.2	B1–5	1_1a, 1_2	All, particularly 6
6.3.9, 6.2	B12,13	1_1b,3_3,3_4	4–14, partic 12 & 13
6.3.6	B11,17	$3_1a,c,a$	All, partic 7
7.3	B6,7	1_1c	6,8
6.3.4, 9.17 7.2, 8.2.5	B8,9,23	1_4	3,6,9,14
6.3.3, 9.1	A15,16	$1_3a,b,c$	6,9,14
6.3.7	A19,10 B18	3_1b	6,10,11,14
6.3.8, 7.11	B14	3_1e	8,14
6.3.10	B20	3_1a	10
6.3.6	B19	3_2	9,14
6.3.5, 6.3.15 3.5, 4.1	B15,A4	2.1*a*,2	2,3
6.3.13	A12	$2_{2.2}$,4.1,4.2	3
6.3.12, 6.3.15 6.3.16, 7.4	A4,A14	4.1	4,9,14
6.3.11	A3,A7	4.1,4.2	2,3,4,5
6.3.14	A15,A16	2,3	2,3,14
6.3.14, 4.1	A17		2,3,4,14
8.2	A6,A18		3,9,14
Aim 4	A1,A2		Especially 2,3,4,14
1.3, 2.3	A5	4.2	2,4,9,11
Aim 5	A17		2,3,4,11,14

Key

ABC *A Basis for Choice* (FEU) 1982

RSA Practical Profile Schemes (Royal Society of Arts) 1983

C&G Communication Skills (City & Guilds) 1981–83